# JAPANESE

## Phrase Book & Dictionary

**Akiko Motoyoshi**
**Michael Houser**

Published by BBC Active, an imprint of Educational Publishers LLP, part of the
Pearson Education Group, Edinburgh Gate, Harlow, Essex CM20 2JE, England.

© Educational Publishers LLP 2007

First published 2007.
Tenth impression 2016.

ISBN: 978-1-4066-1209-7

Cover design: Two Associates
Cover photograph: DAJ/Alamy
Insides design: Pentacor book design
Layout: Oxford Designers & Illustrators
Illustrations © Joanna Kerr, New Division
Language consultant: Yuko Hashimoto
Series editor: Philippa Goodrich
Development manager: Tara Dempsey
Senior production controller: Man Fai Lau

Printed in Malaysia (CTP-VVP).

# how to use this book

This book is divided into colour-coded sections to help you find the language you need as quickly as possible. You can also refer to the **contents** on pages 4–5, and the contents lists at the start of each section.

Along with travel and language tips, each section contains:

 **YOU MAY WANT TO SAY...**
language you'll need for every situation

 **YOU MAY SEE...**
words and phrases you'll see on signs or in print

 **YOU MAY HEAR...** questions, instructions or information people may ask or give you

On page 12 you'll find **essentials**, a list of basic, all-purpose phrases to help you start communicating straight away.

Many of the phrases can be adapted by simply using another word from the dictionary. For instance, take the question 駅はどこですか? *eki wa doko des ka* (Where is the station?). If you want to know where a toilet is, just substitute お手洗い *otearai* for *eki* to give お手洗いはどこですか? *otearai wa doko des ka*.

The **pronunciation guide** is based on English sounds, and is explained on page 6. If you want some guidance on how the Japanese language works, see **basic grammar** on page 191.

The **English-Japanese dictionary** is on page 197.

We welcome any comments or suggestions about this book, but in the meantime, have a good trip – 気を付けて行っていらっしゃい。 *ki o tsukete itte irasshai.*

# contents

## sightseeing &activities   127

## shops &services   147

## health&safety   167

## basic grammar   191

## English – Japanese dictionary   197

# pronunciation guide

Pronunciation of Japanese sounds is very regular. Japanese words are built on combinations of sounds (a consonant plus a vowel), not the sounds of individual letters (with the exception of 'n' and single vowel sounds). For example, 'tomato' is written as トマト in Japanese. It isn't one word to a Japanese speaker, but is split into three sound units: *to*, *ma* and *to*.

(see **sound chart** page 8)

Writing Japanese in roman letters, called *romaji*, means that Japanese sounds cannot be perfectly represented. When you read *romaji* think of it as Japanese, with a Japanese pronunciation. Referring to the sound chart, for example, what looks like the English word 'same' is actually the Japanese word さめ (meaning 'shark' and pronounced *sa me*).

There is no stress within a word when you speak Japanese, all sounds, known as *kana*, are pronounced equally. Japanese words do use pitch to differentiate words that sound similar but are written differently and have different meanings.

## ✳ romaji

We have slightly adapted the way Japanese is written using roman letters.

- There is no real sound like an English 'r' in spoken Japanese. When pronouncing ら, り, る, れ, ろ, the sound shifts between 'l' and 'r'. In this book we use the conventional romaji representation, 'r', e.g. ra, ri, ru, re and ro.

- if a particular vowel sound is 'long', we show this either by doubling the vowel or adding 'h' after a vowel sound. For example, 空港 (くうこう), meaning 'airport', is written as *kuukoh*, and 郵便局 (ゆうびんきょく), meaning 'post office', is written as *yuubin kyoku*.

- ん is the only sound that doesn't include a vowel. It can be pronounced in several ways, the three dominant sounds are 'n', 'ng' and 'm'. ん is pronounced differently depending on what sound follows next. In this book each of these individual sounds is shown as 'n'.

- When は, へ and を are used as particles, they are written as 'wa', 'e' and 'o'.

## ✳ vowels

The natural order for vowels in Japanese is a, i, u, e, o, not, as in English, a, e, i, o, u. Japanese vowels are softer and 'pure', try to produce the sounds not from the back of your throat but at the front of your mouth.

## ✳ double consonants

When pronouncing a double consonant, pause after the first vowel sound before pronouncing the next sound. E.g. ざっし (*zasshi*) meaning 'magazine', pause between the 'za' sound and 'shi' sound.

The chart on the following pages shows how Japanese sounds are broken down in *hiragana* and *katatana*. *Hiragana* is on the second row, *katakana* on the bottom row.

# ✳ sound chart

| a | i | u | e | o |
|---|---|---|---|---|
| あ | い | う | え | お |
| ア | イ | ウ | エ | オ |

| ka | ki | ku | ke | ko |
|---|---|---|---|---|
| か | き | く | け | こ |
| カ | キ | ク | ケ | コ |

| ga | gi | gu | ge | go |
|---|---|---|---|---|
| が | ぎ | ぐ | げ | ご |
| ガ | ギ | グ | ゲ | ゴ |

| sa | shi | su | se | so |
|---|---|---|---|---|
| さ | し | す | せ | そ |
| サ | シ | ス | セ | ソ |

| za | ji | zu | ze | zo |
|---|---|---|---|---|
| ざ | じ | ず | ぜ | ぞ |
| ザ | ジ | ズ | ゼ | ゾ |

| ta | chi | tsu | te | to |
|---|---|---|---|---|
| た | ち | つ | て | と |
| タ | チ | ツ | テ | ト |

| da | ji | zu | de | do |
|---|---|---|---|---|
| だ | ぢ | づ | で | ど |
| ダ | ヂ | ヅ | デ | ド |

| na | ni | nu | ne | no |
|---|---|---|---|---|
| な | に | ぬ | ね | の |
| ナ | ニ | ヌ | ネ | ノ |

| ha | hi | fu | he | ho |
|---|---|---|---|---|
| は | ひ | ふ | へ | ほ |
| ハ | ヒ | フ | ヘ | ホ |

| ba | bi | bu | be | bo |
|---|---|---|---|---|
| ば | び | ぶ | べ | ぼ |
| バ | ビ | ブ | ベ | ボ |

| ya | yu | yo |
|---|---|---|
| や | ゆ | よ |
| ヤ | ユ | ヨ |

| kya | kyu | kyo |
|---|---|---|
| きゃ | きゅ | きょ |
| キャ | キュ | キョ |

| gya | gyu | gyo |
|---|---|---|
| ぎゃ | ぎゅ | よ |
| ギャ | ギュ | ギョ |

| sha | shu | sho |
|---|---|---|
| しゃ | しゅ | しょ |
| シャ | シュ | ショ |

| ja | ju | jo |
|---|---|---|
| じゃ | じゅ | じょ |
| ジャ | ジュ | ジョ |

| cha | chu | cho |
|---|---|---|
| ちゃ | ちゅ | ちょ |
| チャ | チュ | チョ |

| nya | nyu | nyo |
|---|---|---|
| にゃ | にゅ | にょ |
| ニャ | ニュ | ニョ |

| hya | hyu | hyo |
|---|---|---|
| ひゃ | ひゅ | ひょ |
| ヒャ | ヒュ | ヒョ |

| bya | byu | byo |
|---|---|---|
| びゃ | びゅ | びょ |
| ビャ | ビユ | ビョ |

| pa | pi | pu | pe | po |
|---|---|---|---|---|
| ぱ | ぴ | ぷ | ぺ | ぽ |
| パ | ピ | プ | ペ | ポ |

| pya | pyu | pyo |
|---|---|---|
| ぴゃ | ぴゅ | ぴょ |
| ピャ | ピュ | ピョ |

| ma | mi | mu | me | mo |
|---|---|---|---|---|
| ま | み | む | め | も |
| マ | ミ | ム | メ | モ |

| mya | myu | myo |
|---|---|---|
| みゃ | みゅ | みょ |
| ミャ | ミュ | ミョ |

| ra | ri | ru | re | ro |
|---|---|---|---|---|
| ら | り | る | れ | ろ |
| ラ | リ | ル | レ | ロ |

| rya | ryu | ryo |
|---|---|---|
| りゃ | りゅ | りょ |
| リャ | リュ | リョ |

| wa | | n | | wo |
|---|---|---|---|---|
| わ | | ん | | を |
| ワ | | ン | | ヲ |

# ✳ understanding Japanese characters

Written Japanese uses three different scripts: Chinese characters, *kanji*, and two syllabic scripts, *hiragana* and *katakana*. The Latin alphabet, known as *romaji*, is also used in modern Japanese. Western style numerals and *kanji* are used for numbers. Modern Japanese can be written horizontally, from left-to-right, and, more traditionally, vertically, from right-to-left.

*Hiragana* and *katakana,* collectively known as *kana*, are sets of purely phonetic syllabic characters, each set represents the same sounds on which Japanese is based.

*Kanji*, can be 'read' differently. Most *kanji* have an *on* (Chinese) and a *kun* (native Japanese) 'reading' or pronunciation (called *yomi*). Single *kanji* and *kanji* in Japanese place-names and family names are pronounced using their *kun yomi*. The *kanji* for 'east' 東 is pronounced *higashi* on its own, the *kanji* for 'outside' 外 is pronounced *soto* on its own, both are *kun yomi*. If these same *kanji* are combined with other *kanji* (creating a compound *kanji*), as in 東京 and 外国, their *on yomi* is used. 東京 is pronounced *toh kyoh* ('capital in the east') and 外国 is pronounced *gaikoku* ('foreign countries' or 'outside countries').

## ✳ kanji

About 2,000 characters are deemed necessary for effective daily communication (e.g. reading a newspaper). They represent concepts rather than sounds. Only officially approved *kanji* can be used for names.

## ✳ hiragana

*Hiragana* are used to write Japanese words for which there were no *kanji,* and as endings for *kanji* to show verb and adjective conjugations, this is called *okurigana*. *Hiragana* are also written above or beside *kanji* to show the proper reading, this is *furigana*. There are 46 core *hiragana*.

## ✳ katakana

*Katakana* are used mainly for writing foreign words, names or brands. Also, as the syllables are the same as hiragana Japanese words and names can be written in *katakana* for emphasis. There are 46 core *katakana*.

## ✳ romaji

*Romaji* is often used for road signs, station names etc., generally for use by people who do not read *kanji* or *kana*. It is one of the ways Japanese text can be entered into electronic files.

# the basics

# *essentials

| | | |
|---|---|---|
| How do you do? | はじめまして。 | *hajime mashite* |
| Pleased to meet you. | お目にかかれて嬉しいです。 | *ome ni kakarete ure shii des* |
| How are you? | お元気ですか? | *o genki des ka* |
| I'm/We're fine. | お陰様で, 元気です。 | *okage sama de genki des* |
| Good morning. | お早う。 | *o hayoh* |
| Good morning. (polite) | お早うございます。 | *o hayoh gozai mas* |
| Good day/Good afternoon. | 今日は。 | *kon nichi wa* |
| Good evening. | 今晩は。 | *kon ban wa* |
| Good night. | お休みなさい。 | *oyasumi nasai* |
| Goodbye/Farewell. | さようなら。 | *sayoh nara* |
| Yes. | はい。 | *hai* |
| No. | いいえ。 | *iie* |
| I'm/We're sorry. (formal) | すみません。 申し訳ありません。 | *sumi masen.* *moshi wake arimasen* |
| Pardon me/Excuse me/us. (formal) | すみません。 失礼します。 | *sumimasen* *shitsurei shimas* |
| Thank you (very much). | どうもありがとう (ございます)。 | *dohmo arigatoh (gozaimas)* |
| You're welcome./ Don't mention it. | どう致しまして。 | *doh itashi mashite* |

the basics

| | | |
|---|---|---|
| I don't understand. | 分かりません。 | *wakarimasen* |
| I only speak a little Japanese. | 日本語は少ししか話せません。 | *nihongo wa sukoshi shika hanase masen* |
| May I speak in English? | 英語で話してもよろしいですか? | *eigo de hanashitemo yoroshii des ka* |
| Does anyone speak English? | どなたか英語が話せますか? | *donata ka eigo ga hanase mas ka* |
| Could you repeat that, please? | すみませんが、もう一度お願いします? | *sumimasen ga moh ichido onegai shimas* |
| More slowly, please. | もう少しゆっくりお願いします。 | *moh sukoshi yukkuri onegai shimas* |
| How do you say it/that in Japanese? | それは日本語で何ですか? | *sorewa nihongo de nan des ka* |
| When...? | いつですか? | *itsu des ka* |
| What is/are this/these? | これは何ですか? | *kore wa nan des ka* |
| How much is/are it/those? | それはいくらですか? | *sore wa ikura des ka* |
| Where is/are...? | …はどこですか? | *...wa doko des ka* |
| Show it to me on the map, please. | 地図のどこか教えて下さい。 | *chizu no doko ka oshiete kudasai* |
| Help! | 助けて! | *tasu keteh!* |

## ✳ numbers

● Both western and Japanese scripts (*kanji*) are used
for numbers throughout Japan. There are specific *kanji*
'counters' for units of 1,000 千 *(sen)*, 10,000 万 *(man)* and
100,000,000 億 *(oku)*. For example, instead of a single *kanji*
number for 50,000, the *kanji* number is 五万, literally 5 units
of 10,000.

| 0 | 零/ゼロ | *rei/zero* |
|---|---|---|
| 1 | 一 | *ichi* |
| 2 | 二 | *ni* |
| 3 | 三 | *san* |
| 4 | 四 | *yon/shi* |
| 5 | 五 | *go* |
| 6 | 六 | *roku* |
| 7 | 七 | *nana/shichi* |
| 8 | 八 | *hachi* |
| 9 | 九 | *kyuu/ku* |
| 10 | 十 | *juu* |
| 11 | 十一 | *juu ichi* |
| 12 | 十二 | *juu ni* |
| 13 | 十三 | *juu san* |
| 14 | 十四 | *juu yon/juushi* |
| 15 | 十五 | *juu go* |
| 16 | 十六 | *juu roku* |
| 17 | 十七 | *juu nana/juu shichi* |
| 18 | 十八 | *juu hachi* |
| 19 | 十九 | *juu kyuu/juu ku* |
| 20 | 二十 | *ni juu* |
| 21 | 二十一 | *ni juu ichi* |
| 22... | 二十二… | *ni juu ni…* |

| | | |
|---|---|---|
| 30 | 三十 | *san juu* |
| 31 | 三十一 | *san juu ichi* |
| 32... | 三十二… | *san juu ni…* |
| 40 | 四十 | *yon juu* |
| 50 | 五十 | *go juu* |
| 60 | 六十 | *roku juu* |
| 70 | 七十 | *nana juu* |
| 80 | 八十 | *hachi juu* |
| 90 | 九十 | *kyuu juu* |
| 100 | 百 | *hyaku* |
| 101 | 百一 | *hyaku ichi* |
| 102... | 百二… | *hyaku ni…* |
| 200 | 二百 | *ni hyaku* |
| 250 | 二百五十 | *ni hyaku go juu* |
| 300 | 三百 | *san byaku* |
| 400 | 四百 | *yon hyaku* |
| 500 | 五百 | *go hyaku* |
| 600 | 六百 | *roppyaku* |
| 700 | 七百 | *nana hyaku* |
| 800 | 八百 | *happyaku* |
| 900 | 九百 | *kyuu hyaku* |
| 1,000 | 千 | *sen* |
| 2,000 | 二千 | *ni sen* |
| 3,000 | 三千 | *san zen* |
| 4,000 | 四千 | *yon sen* |
| 5,000 | 五千 | *go sen* |
| 10,000 | 一万 | *ichi man* |
| 100,000 | 十万 | *juu man* |
| one million | 百万 | *hyaku man* |
| one and a half million | 百五十万 | *hyaku go juu man* |
| 100 million | 一億 | *ichi oku* |

## ✳ numbers for counting things

(see **basic grammar**, page 195)

| | | |
|---|---|---|
| 1 | ひとつ | *hitotsu* |
| 2 | ふたつ | *futatsu* |
| 3 | みっつ | *mittsu* |
| 4 | よっつ | *yottsu* |
| 5 | いつつ | *itsutsu* |
| 6 | むっつ | *muttsu* |
| 7 | ななつ | *nanatsu* |
| 8 | やっつ | *yattsu* |
| 9 | ここのつ | *kokonotsu* |
| 10 | とお | *toh* |

● Japanese dates are expressed as 'suns'; the 15th of the month is 十五日 (*juugo nichi*) or 'fifteen suns'.

| | | |
|---|---|---|
| first | 一日 | *tsu i ta chi* |
| second | 二日 | *futsuka* |
| third | 三日 | *mikka* |
| fourth | 四日 | *yokka* |
| fifth | 五日 | *itsu ka* |
| sixth | 六日 | *mui ka* |
| seventh | 七日 | *nano ka* |
| eighth | 八日 | *yoh ka* |
| ninth | 九日 | *kokono ka* |
| tenth | 十日 | *toh ka* |
| eleventh | 十一日 | *juu ichi nichi* |
| twelfth | 十二日 | *juu ni nichi* |
| thirteenth | 十三日 | *juu san nichi* |
| fourteenth | 十四日 | *juu yokka* |
| fifteenth | 十五日 | *juu go nichi* |

| sixteenth | 十六日 | *juu roku nichi* |
|---|---|---|
| seventeenth | 十七日 | *juu nana nichi* |
| eighteenth | 十八日 | *juu hachi nichi* |
| nineteenth | 十九日 | *juu ku nichi* |
| twentieth | 二十日 | *hatsuka* |
| twenty-first | 二十一日 | *ni juu ichi nichi* |
| twenty-second | 二十二日 | *ni juu ni nichi* |
| twenty-third | 二十三日 | *ni juu san nichi* |
| twenty-fourth | 二十四日 | *ni juu yokka* |
| twenty-fifth... | 二十五日 | *ni juu go nichi* |
| twenty-ninth | 二十九日 | *ni juu ku nichi* |
| thirtieth | 三十日 | *san juu nichi* |
| thirty-first | 三十一日 | *san juu ichi nichi* |

## ✳ ages

| 1 year old | 一歳／１才 | *issai* |
|---|---|---|
| 2 years old | 二歳／２才 | *ni sai* |
| 3 years old | 三歳／３才 | *san sai* |
| 4 years old | 四歳／４才 | *yon sai* |
| 5 years old | 五歳／５才 | *go sai* |
| 6 years old | 六歳／６才 | *roku sai* |
| 7 years old | 七歳／７才 | *nana sai* |
| 8 years old | 八歳／８才 | *hassai* |
| 9 years old | 九歳／９才 | *kyuu sai* |
| 10 years old | 十歳／１０才 | *jussai* |
| 11 years old | 十一歳／１１才 | *juu issai* |
| 12 years old... | 十二歳／１２才 | *juu ni sai* |
| 18 years old | 十八歳／１８才 | *juu hassai* |
| 19 years old | 十九歳／１９才 | *juu kyuu sai* |
| 20 years old | 二十歳／２０才 | *hatachi/ni jussai* |

| 21 years old | 二十一歳／２１才 | *ni juu issai* |
| 22 years old... | 二十二歳／２２才 | *ni juu ni sai* |
| 30 years old | 三十歳／３０才 | *san jussai* |
| 31 years old | 三十一歳／３１才 | *san juu issai* |
| 32 years old... | 三十二歳／３２才 | *san juu ni sai* |

## ✳ fractions

● Japanese fractions are expressed back-to-front from a Western perspective. 1/3, in Japanese (三分の一) is, effectively, 'three parts of one'.

| a quarter | 四分の一 | *yon bun no ichi* |
| a half | 二分の一／半分 | *ni bun no ichi/han bun* |
| three-quarters | 四分の三 | *yon bun no san* |
| a third | 三分の一 | *san bun no ichi* |
| two-thirds | 三分の二 | *san bun no ni* |

## ✳ days

● Many Japanese days of the week are expressed as a natural element plus 'sun' 日 (representing 'day'). For example Tuesday is 'fire day' 火曜日 *(ka yohbi)*; Wednesday is 'water day' 水曜日 *(sui yohbi)*. Only Sunday 日曜日 *(nichi yohbi)* literally 'sun day' and Monday 月曜日 *(getsu yohbi)*, 'moon day' directly parallel western days of the week.

| Monday    | 月曜日 | *getsu yohbi* |
| Tuesday   | 火曜日 | *ka yohbi* |
| Wednesday | 水曜日 | *sui yohbi* |
| Thursday  | 木曜日 | *moku yohbi* |
| Friday    | 金曜日 | *kin yohbi* |
| Saturday  | 土曜日 | *do yohbi* |
| Sunday    | 日曜日 | *nichi yohbi* |

## ✳ months

| January   | 一月   | *ichi gatsu* |
| February  | 二月   | *ni gatsu* |
| March     | 三月   | *san gatsu* |
| April     | 四月   | *shi gatsu* |
| May       | 五月   | *go gatsu* |
| June      | 六月   | *roku gatsu* |
| July      | 七月   | *shichi gatsu* |
| August    | 八月   | *hachi gatsu* |
| September | 九月   | *ku gatsu* |
| October   | 十月   | *juu gatsu* |
| November  | 十一月 | *juu ichi gatsu* |
| December  | 十二月 | *juu ni gatsu* |

## ✳ seasons

| spring | 春 | *haru* |
| summer | 夏 | *natsu* |
| autumn | 秋 | *aki* |
| winter | 冬 | *fuyu* |

the basics

## ✳ dates

| | | |
|---|---|---|
| ● **What day is it today?** | 今日は何曜日ですか。 | *kyoh wa nan yohbi des ka* |
| ● **What date is it today?** | 今日は何日ですか。 | *kyoh wa nan nichi des ka* |
| ● **When is...** | …はいつですか | *... wa itsu des ka* |
| **your birthday?** | （あなたの）誕生日 | *(anata no) tan jyohbi* |
| ● **(It's) the fifteenth of April.** | 四月十五日/４月１５日です。 | *shi gatsu juu go nichi des* |

## ✳ telling the time

● Japanese travel timetables work on a 24-hour clock; otherwise, time is expressed in 12-hour units, in terms of am and pm. 10am is 午前十時 *(go zen juu ji)*, 10pm is 午後十時 *(go go juu ji)*.

| | | |
|---|---|---|
| ● **What time is it?** | 何時ですか。 | *nan ji des ka* |
| ● **What time does it...** | 何時に…ますか | *nan ji ni ... mas ka* |
| **open?/close?** | 開き/閉まり | *aki/shimari* |
| **start?/finish?** | 始まり/終わり | *hajimarii/owari* |
| ● **am** | 午前 | *go zen* |
| ● **pm** | 午後 | *go go* |

- It's...　　　　　　…です　　　　　　…des
  - 10 o'clock　　　十時／１０時　　　juu ji
  - midday　　　　　正午　　　　　　shoh go
  - midnight　　　　真夜中　　　　　ma yonaka

- at...　　　　　　…に　　　　　　…ni
  - half-past nine　　九時半／9時半　　ku ji han
  - quarter past　　　九時十五分／　　ku ji juu go fun
    nine　　　　　　　9時１５分
  - quarter to ten　　十時十五分前／　juu ji juu go fun
    　　　　　　　　10時１５分前　　mae
  - twenty past　　　十時二十分／１０時　juu ji ni juppun
    ten　　　　　　　　２０分
  - twenty-five to　　十時二十五分前／　juu ji ni juu go fun
    ten　　　　　　　10時２５分前　　mae
  - precisely ten　　十時ちょうど／　　juu ji choh do
    o'clock　　　　　10時ちょうど

- in...　　　　　　…で　　　　　　…de
  - ten minutes　　　十分／１０分　　　ju pun
  - half an hour　　　三十分／３０分　　san juppun
  - an hour　　　　　一時間／1時間　　ichi jikan

## ✳ time phrases

- day　　　　　　日　　　　　nichi/hi/jitsu
- week　　　　　週　　　　　shuu
- fortnight　　　二週間　　　ni shuu kan
- month　　　　月　　　　　tsuki/gatsu
- year　　　　　年　　　　　toshi/nen

the basics

| | | |
|---|---|---|
| today | 今日 | *kyoh* |
| tomorrow | あした | *ashita* |
| the day after tomorrow | あさって | *asatte* |
| yesterday | きのう | *kinoh* |
| the day before yesterday | おととい | *ototoi* |
| this morning | 今朝 | *kesa* |
| this afternoon | 今日の午後 | *kyoh no gogo* |
| this evening | 今晩 | *konban* |
| tonight | 今夜 | *konya* |
| on Friday/s | 金曜日に | *kin yohbi ni* |
| every Friday | 毎週金曜日に | *maishu kin yohbi ni* |
| every...<br>　day<br>　week<br>　month<br>　year | 毎…<br>　日<br>　週<br>　月<br>　年 | *mai...*<br>　*nichi*<br>　*shuu*<br>　*tsuki*<br>　*toshi* |
| for...<br>　a week<br>　two weeks<br>　two years<br>　a month | …間<br>　一週/1週<br>　二週/2週<br>　二年/2年<br>　一か月/1か月 | *...kan*<br>　*isshuu*<br>　*ni shuu*<br>　*ni nen*<br>　*ikka getsu* |
| I'm here for two weeks. | 二週間ここにいます。 | *ni shuu kan koko ni imas* |
| I've been here for a month. | 一か月間ここにいます。 | *ikka getsu kan koko ni imas* |

| | | |
|---|---|---|
| I've been studying Japanese for two years. | 二年間日本語を勉強しています。 | *ni nen kan nihongo o benkyoh shite imas* |
| next... | 来… | *rai...* |
|   week | 週 | *shuu* |
|   month | 月 | *getsu* |
|   year | 年 | *nen* |
|   spring | 春 | *shun* |
| last night | きのうの晩 | *kinoh no ban* |
| last year | 去年/昨年 | *kyo nen/saku nen* |
| last... | 先… | *sen...* |
|   week | 週 | *shuu* |
|   month | 月 | *getsu* |
| a few days ago | 先日 | *sen jitsu* |
| a week ago | 一週間前/1週間前 | *isshuu kan mae* |
| a year ago | 一年前/1 年前 | *ichi nen mae* |
| since... | …から | *...kara* |
|   yesterday | きのう | *kinoh* |
|   last week | 先週 | *sen shuu* |
|   last month | 先月 | *sen getsu* |
|   last year | 去年/昨年 | *kyo nen/saku nen* |
| (in) the morning/ afternoon | 午前中（に）/ 午後（に） | *go zen chuu (ni)/ gogo (ni)* |
| in six months' time | 半年の内に/六か月以内に | *han toshi no uchi ni/rokka getsu inai ni* |
| at night | 夜に | *yoru ni* |
| It's... | …です | *...des* |
|   early | （まだ）早い | *(mada) hayai* |
|   late | 遅い/間に合わない | *osoi/ma ni awanai* |

# ✳ measurements

● Japan uses the metric system for weights and measurements. Distance is in kilometres; weight in grammes and kilos; clothing in centimetres. When expressing internal housing space, or field sizes, the joh 畳 [1.65 m²] and tsubo 坪 [3.3 m²] are used. 1 joh is the area of a tatami mat, traditional flooring still used in Japanese homes.

| | | |
|---|---|---|
| millimetres | ミリメートル/mm | *miri mehtoru* |
| centimetres | センチメートル/cm | *senchi mehtoru* |
| metres | メートル/m | *mehtoru* |
| kilometres | キロメートル/km | *kiro mehtoru* |
| miles | マイル | *mai ru* |
| millilitres | ミリリットル/ml | *miri rittoru* |
| a litre | 1リットル/l | *ichi rittoru* |
| 25 litres | 25リットル | *ni juu go rittoru* |
| gramme | グラム/g | *guramu* |
| 100 grammes | 100グラム | *hyaku guramu* |
| 200 grammes | 200グラム | *ni hyaku guramu* |
| kilo/s | キロ（グラム）/kg | *kiro(guramu)* |

## CONVERSIONS

**1km** = 0.62 miles
**1 mile** = 1.61km
**1 litre** = 1.8 pints
**100g** = 3.5oz
**1oz** = 28g
**1lb** = 450g

**200g** = 7oz
**¼lb** = 113g
**½ kilo** = 1.1 lb
**½lb** = 225g
**1 kilo** = 2.2 lb

To convert kilometres to miles, divide by 8 and multiply by 5 e.g. 16 kilometres (16/8 = 2, 2 × 5 = 10) = 10 miles.

For miles to kilometres, divide by 5 and multiply by 8 e.g. 50 miles (50/5 = 10, 10 × 8 = 80) = 80 kilometres.

## ✳ clothes and shoe sizes

**WOMEN'S CLOTHES**

| UK | 6 | 8 | 10 | 12 | 14 | 16 | 18 | 20 |
|---|---|---|---|---|---|---|---|---|
| Japan | 7 | 9 | 11 | 13 | 15 | 17 | 19 | 21 |

**MEN'S CLOTHES**

| UK | 34–36 | 38–40 | 42–44 | 46 |
|---|---|---|---|---|
| Japan | S | M | L | LL |

**MEN'S SHIRTS**

| UK | 14 | 14½ | 15 | 15½ | 16 | 16½ | 17 |
|---|---|---|---|---|---|---|---|
| Japan | 36 | 37 | 38 | 39 | 40 | 41 | 42 |

**CHILDREN'S CLOTHES**

| UK (in) | 43 | 48 | 55 | 58 | 60 |
|---|---|---|---|---|---|
| Japan (cm) | 125 | 135 | 150 | 155 | 160 |

**WOMEN'S SHOES**

| UK | 4 | 4½ | 5 | 5½ | 6 | 6½ | 7½ |
|---|---|---|---|---|---|---|---|
| Japan (cm) | 22½ | 23 | 23½ | 24 | 24½ | 25 | 25½ |

**MEN'S SHOES**

| UK | 7 | 8 | 9 | 10 | 11 |
|---|---|---|---|---|---|
| Japan (cm) | 26 | 26½ | 27½ | 28 | 29 |

the basics

## ✳ false friends

● Like many languages, Japanese borrows words from other languages. These are called 外来語 *(gairaigo)* literally language coming from outside. *Gairaigo* is easily recognisable since the words are always written in *katakana*.

● *Gairaigo* consists of words for which no Japanese term exists エスカレーター *(esuka reitan)* 'escalator'; インターネット *(intahnetto)* 'internet', or, increasingly, to add a buzz to an existing Japanese concept or product カラオケ *(karaoke)*, 'empty orchestra'. The words are borrowed from many languages, with English being the most popular.

● Often the borrowed words are abbreviated, e.g. personal computer becomes パソコン *(pasokon* from *pahsonaru konpyuuta)*.

| JAPANESE USAGE | NOT TO BE CONFUSED WITH... |
|---|---|
| アベック *(abekku)* **couple** | **avec** (in French) |
| アルバイト *(arubaito)* **part-time job** | **arbeit** (in German) |
| マンション *(manshon)* **flat** | **mansion** |
| サービス *(sahbisu)* **free-of-charge** | **service** |

# ✳ national holidays and festivals

● Japan has a large number of secular national holidays. 'Golden Week', in late April/early May, has the largest concentration of public holidays. New Year is one of the main family holidays. Christmas isn't an official holiday.

● There are also various festivals 祭 *(matsuri)* all over Japan, usually commemorating the changing of the seasons, historical events or symbolising religious rituals. Among the most famous *matsuri* are: the *Gion Matsuri*, which has taken place in Kyoto every July since 970 AD; the world-famous *Yuki Matsuri* or Snow Festival, held in Sapporo in early February. *O-bon* is a traditional Buddhist holiday in mid-August commemorating ancestors. Japan's biggest pop festival, *Fuji rokku* (Fujirock), is held during the last weekend in July.

● Japan has adopted Valentine's day and added its own twist: on 14th February, females give brown chocolate – to bosses and *koibito* (lovers), while on 14th March (White Day) men give women white chocolate.

| 元日 | gan jitsu | New Year's Day: 1 January |
| 成人の日 | sei jin no hi | Coming-of-Age Day: 2nd Monday in January |
| 建国記念日 | ken koku kinen bi | National Foundation Day: 11 February |
| 春分の日 | shun bun no hi | Spring Equinox: in March, varies annually |
| 昭和の日 | shoh wa no hi | Showa Memorial Day: 29 April |
| 憲法記念日 | ken poh kinen bi | Constitution Day: 3 May |
| みどりの日 | midori no hi | Environment Day: 4 May |
| こどもの日 | kodomo no hi | Children's Day: 5 May |
| 海の日 | u mi no hi | Marine Day: 3rd Monday in July |
| 敬老の日 | kei roh no hi | Respect-for-the-Aged Day: 3rd Monday in September |
| 秋分の日 | shuu bun no hi | Autumn Equinox: in September, varies annually |
| 体育の日 | tai iku no hi | Sports Day: 2nd Monday in October |
| 文化の日 | bunka no hi | Culture Day: 3 November |
| 勤労感謝の日 | kinroh kansha no hi | Labour Day: 23 November |
| 天皇誕生日 | ten noh tan joh bi | Emperor's Birthday: 23 December |

# general conversation

# ✳ greetings

- **Good morning.**
  (polite form)

  お早う。
  お早うございます。

  *ohayoh*
  *ohayoh gozaimas*

- **Good day.**

  今日は。

  *kon nichi wa*

- **Good evening.**

  今晩は。

  *kon ban wa*

- **Good night.**
  (polite form)

  お休み。
  お休みなさい。

  *oyasumi*
  *oyasumi nasai*

- **Goodbye/Bye/
  Farewell.**

  さようなら。

  *sayoh nara*

- **See you later.**
  (informal)

  では、また。
  じゃあ、また。

  *dewa, mata*
  *ja, mata*

- **How do you do?**

  はじめまして。

  *hajime mashite*

- **How are you?**
  (informal)

  お元気ですか。
  元気。

  *o genki des ka?*
  *genki?*

- **Fine, thanks.**

  はい、おかげさまで。

  *hai, okage sama de*

- **And you?**

  お変わりありませ
  んか。

  *okawari arimasen ka?*

# ✳ introductions

The Japanese custom is to introduce yourself with your surname first. When introducing yourself, no form of address is used; when addressing or referring to others, add the suffix *san* (さん) to the end of the name. *San* can be used with male or female names (both first and surname), and almost any age.

For children use *chan* (ちゃん) at the end of the first names of young children, and *kun* (君) at the end of either the first name or surname of teenagers, especially boys.

## YOU MAY WANT TO SAY...

| | | |
|---|---|---|
| • **My name is...** | 私の名前は … です | *watashi no namae wa … des* |
| • **My (family) name is...** | 私の名字は … です | *watashi no myohji wa … des* |
| • **This is...** (referring to a man) | こちらは … です | *kochira wa ... des* |
| **Mr Brown** | ブラウンさん | *bura u n san* |
| **my husband** | （私の）夫 | *(watashi no) otto* |
| **my son** | （私の）息子 | *(watashi no) musuko* |
| **my fiancé** | （私の）婚約者 | *(watashi no) kon yakusha* |
| **my boyfriend** | （私の）恋人/彼 | *(watashi no) koibito/kare* |
| • **This is...** (referring to a woman) | こちらは … です | *kochira wa ... des* |
| **Miss/Mrs Brown** | ブラウンさん | *bura u n san* |
| **my wife** | （私の）妻 | *(watashi no) tsuma* |
| **my daughter** | （私の）娘 | *(watashi no) musume* |
| **my fiancée** | （私の）婚約者 | *(watashi no) kon yaku sha* |
| **my girlfriend** | （私の）恋人/彼女 | *(watashi no) koi bito/kanojo* |
| **my female friend** | （私の）女友だち/友だち | *(watashi no) onna tomo dachi/tomo dachi* |
| • **I'm pleased to meet you.** | お目にかかれて嬉しく思います。 | *omeni kakarete ureshiku omoi mas* |

## ✳ talking about yourself

| | | |
|---|---|---|
| I'm British. | （私は）イギリス人です。 | *(watashi wa) igirisu jin des* |
| I'm Irish. | （私は）アイルランド人です。 | *(watashi wa) airurando jin des* |
| I come from... | （私は）… 出身です | *(watashi wa) ... shusshin des* |
| England | イングランド | *ingurando* |
| Ireland | アイルランド | *airurando* |
| Scotland | スコットランド | *sukottorando* |
| Wales | ウェールズ | *uehruzu* |
| I/We live in... | （私/私たちは）… に住んでいます | *(watashi/watashi tachi wa) ... ni su nde imas* |
| London | ロンドン | *rondon* |
| Edinburgh | エディンバラ | *ejinbara* |
| I'm 25 years old. | （私は）二十五歳です。 | *(watashi wa) nijuu go sai des* |
| I'm a... | 私は … です | *watashi wa ... des* |
| web designer | ウェブデザイナー | *uebu dezainah* |
| student | 学生 | *gakusei* |
| I work in/for... | 私は … で働いています | *watashi wa ... de hataraite imas* |
| a bank | 銀行 | *ginkoh* |
| I'm retired. | （私は）定年退職しました。 | *(watashi wa) tei nen tai shoku shimashita* |
| I'm self-employed. | （私は）自営業です。 | *(watashi wa) jiei gyoh des* |

| | | |
|---|---|---|
| I'm married. | （私は）結婚しています。 | (watashi wa) kekkon shite imas |
| I'm...<br>divorced<br>single<br>a widow/<br>widower | （私は）… です<br>離婚しています<br>独身<br>未亡人/男やもめ | (watashi wa) ... des<br>rikon shiteimas<br>dokushin<br>miboh jin/otoko<br>yamome |
| I have...<br>three children<br>one brother<br>two sisters | 私には … います<br>子供が三人<br>兄弟が一人<br>姉妹が二人 | watashi niwa ... imas<br>kodomo ga san nin<br>kyodai ga hitori<br>shimai ga futami |
| I don't have...<br>any children<br>any brothers or<br>sisters | 私には … はいません<br>子供<br>兄弟（姉妹） | watashi niwa ... wa imasen<br>kodomo<br>kyoh dai (shimai) |
| I'm on holiday. | （私は）休暇でここに来ています。 | (watashi wa) kyuuka de koko ni kiteimas |
| I'm here on business. | （私は）ここに仕事で来ています。 | (watashi wa) koko ni shigoto de kiteimas |
| I'm here with my...<br><br>family<br>colleague | （私は）… と一緒にここに来ています<br><br>家族<br>同僚 | (watashi wa) ... to isshoni koko ni kite imas<br>kazoku<br>doh ryoh |
| My husband/son is... | （私の）夫/息子は … です。 | (watashi no) otto/musuko wa ... des |
| My wife/daughter is... | （私の）妻/娘は … です。 | (watashi no) tsuma/musume wa ... des |

## ✳ asking about other people

| | | |
|---|---|---|
| What's your name? | お名前は何ですか。 | onamae wa nan des ka? |
| Where do you come from? | どちらのご出身ですか。 | dochira no go shushin des ka? |
| Are you married? | 結婚していますか。 | kekkon shite imas ka? |
| Do you have... any children? any brothers and sisters? a girlfriend/ boyfriend? | …はいますか。 お子さん ご兄弟（姉妹） 彼女/彼 | ...wa imas ka? oko san go kyohdai (shimai) kanojyo/kare |
| How old are you? | おいくつですか。 | oikutsu des ka? |
| Is this your... husband/wife? boyfriend/ girlfriend? friend? | こちらは … ですか ご主人/奥さん 彼/彼女 友人/友だち | kochira wa ... des ka? goshujinn/okusan kare/kanojo yuu jin/tomodachi |
| Where are you going? | どちらへお出かけですか。 | dochira e odekake des ka? |
| Where are you staying? | どこに滞在していますか。 | doko ni taizai shite imas ka? |
| Where do you live? | どこに住んでいますか。 | doko ni sunde imas ka? |
| What do you do? | お仕事は何ですか。 | oshigoto wa nan des ka? |
| What are you studying? | 何を勉強していますか。 | nani o benkyoh shite imas ka? |

general conversation

# ✳ chatting

- Kyoto is very beautiful.

  京都はとてもきれいです。

  *kyoto wa totemo kirei des*

- I like Japan (very much).

  （私は）日本が（とても）好きです。

  *(watashi wa) nihon ga (totemo)ski des*

- It's the first time I've been to...

  （私は）… は初めてです。

  *(watashi wa)... wa hajimete des*

- I come to Tokyo often.

  （私は）東京によく来ます。

  *(watashi wa) tohkyoh ni yoku kimas*

- Do you live here?

  こちらにお住まいですか。

  *kochira ni osumai des ka?*

- Are you from here?

  こちらの　ご出身ですか。

  *kochira no go shushin des ka?*

- Have you ever been to...

  … に行ったことがありますか

  *...ni itta koto ga arimas ka?*

  - Britain?
    
    イギリス
    
    *igirisu*
  - London?
    
    ロンドン
    
    *rondon*
  - the Lake District?
    
    湖水地方
    
    *kosui chihoh*

- Did you like it?

  気に入りましたか。

  *ki ni iri mashita ka?*

| …が好きですか。 | *...ga ski des ka?* | Do you like...? |
| どのくらいこちらにいらっしゃいますか。 | *donokurai kochira ni irasshai mas ka?* | How long are you here for? |

general conversation

| 日本語がとても上手ですね。 | *nihongo ga totemo johzu des ne* | You speak Japanese very well. |
| おはしが使えますか。 | *Ohashi ga tsukaemas ka?* | Can you use chopsticks? |
| …をどう思いますか。 | *...o doh omoi mas ka?* | What do you think of...? |

## ✳ the weather

### YOU MAY WANT TO SAY...

| It's... | … です | *...des* |
| a beautiful day! | すがすがしい日 | *suga suga shii hi* |
| a beautiful morning! | すがすがしい朝 | *suga suga shii asa* |
| What fantastic weather! | いい天気です。 | *ii tenki des* |
| It's (very)... | （とても） … です | *(totemo) ... des* |
| hot | 暑い | *atsui* |
| cold | 寒い | *samui* |
| windy | 風が強い | *kaze ga tsuyoi* |
| What's the forecast... | … 天気予報は何ですか。 | *...tenki yohoh wa nan des ka?* |
| for Sunday? | 一日曜日の | *nichiyoh bi no* |
| for tomorrow? | 明日の | *ashita no/asu no* |
| It's ... today | 今日は … です | *kyoh wa ... des* |
| Tuesday | 火曜日 | *kayoh bi* |
| fine | 晴れ | *hare* |
| cloudy | 曇り | *kumori* |
| It's... | … が降っています | *...ga futte imas* |
| raining | 雨 | *ame* |
| snowing | 雪 | *yuki* |

## likes and dislikes, feelings and opinions

### ✳ likes and dislikes

- I like...
  sake

  … が好きです
  日本酒

  ...ga ski des
  nihon shu

- I love...
  sushi

  … がとても好きです
  すし

  ...ga totemo ski des
  sushi

- I don't like...

  …が好きじゃあり
  ません

  ...ga ski ja arima sen

  tomatoes

  トマト

  tomato

- I hate...
  fermented
  soybeans

  …が嫌いです
  納豆

  ...ga kirai des
  nattoh

- Do you like...
  dogs?
  swimming?

  …が好きですか
  犬
  水泳

  ...ga ski des ka?
  inu
  sui eh

- I like it/them.

  好きです。

  ski des

- I don't like it/
  them.

  好きじゃありませ
  ん。

  ski ja arima sen

### ✳ feelings and opinions

- Are you...
  ok?
  happy?

  …ですか
  大丈夫
  幸せ

  ...des ka?
  dai johbu
  shiawase

- I'm (just)...

  （ちょっと）… だ
  けです

  (chotto) ... dake des

  tired

  疲れた

  tsukareta

| | | |
|---|---|---|
| I'm a bit annoyed. | （私は）ちょっと腹が たちました。 | *(watashi wa) chotto haraga tachi mashita* |
| What do you think of...? | …をどう思います か。 | *...o doh omoi mas ka?* |
| I/We think it's... | （私/私たちは）… と 思います | *(watashi/watashi tachi wa) ... to omoi mas* |
| great | すばらしい | *subarashii* |
| sad | 悲しい | *kana shii* |
| Did you like it? | 気に入りましたか。 | *ki ni iri mashita ka?* |
| I/We thought it was... | （私/私たちは）… と 思いました | *(watashi/watashi tachi wa) ... to omoi mashita* |
| beautiful | きれいだ | *kirei da* |
| awful | ひどい | *hidoi* |
| Don't you like it? | 好きじゃありませんか。 | *ski ja arima sen ka?* |
| Do you like him/ her? | 彼/彼女を気に入りま したか。 | *kare/kanojo o ki ni iri mashita ka?* |
| I like him/her. | 彼/彼女を気に入りま した。 | *kare/kanojo o ki ni iri mashita* |
| What's your favourite... | 好きな … は何で すか | *ski na ... wa nan des ka?* |
| food? | 食べ物 | *tabe mono* |
| Who's your favourite... | 好きな … は誰で すか | *ski na ... wa dare des ka?* |
| actor/actress? | 俳優/女優 | *hai yuu/jo yuu* |
| My favourite... is... | 私の好きな … は … です | *watashi no suki na ... wa ... des* |
| Please go away. | ちょっと、遠慮して いただけませんか | *chotto enryo shite itadake masen ka?* |

# ✱ making arrangements

| | | |
|---|---|---|
| What are you doing tonight? | 今夜は何をする予定ですか。 | *kon ya wa nani o suru yoteh des ka?* |
| Would you like something to eat? | 食事でもいかがですか。 | *shokuji demo ikaga des ka?* |
| Would you like... a drink? to come with us? | …行きませんか 飲みに 私たちと一緒に | *...iki masen ka? nomi ni watashi tachi to issho ni* |
| Yes, I'd love to. | はい、喜んで。 | *hai, yoro kon de* |
| No, thank you. | すみません。 | *sumimasen* |
| Sorry, we already have plans. | 残念ですが、もう予定があります。 | *zan nen desga, moh yoteh ga ari mas* |
| What time shall we meet? | 何時に会いましょうか。 | *nan ji ni aimashoh ka?* |
| Where shall we meet? | どこで会いましょうか。 | *doko de ai mashoh ka?* |
| See you later. | じゃ、また。 | *ja, mata* |
| What's your email address? | メールアドレスを教えて下さい。 | *meiru adoresu o oshiete kudasai* |
| My email address is... @... dot com. | （私の）メールアドレスは … アットマーク … ドット コムです | *(watashi no) meiru adoresu wa ... atto mahku ... dotto komu des* |

general conversation

39

# ✳ useful expressions

● 'Sorry' すみません *(sumimasen)* is also used to say 'thank you'.

(see **essentials**, page 12)

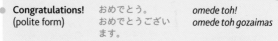

## YOU MAY WANT TO SAY...

| | | |
|---|---|---|
| ● Congratulations! (polite form) | おめでとう。 おめでとうございます。 | *omede toh!* *omede toh gozaimas* |
| ● Happy Birthday! | お誕生日おめでとうございます。 | *o tan joh bi omede toh gozai mas!* |
| ● Happy Christmas! | メリークリスマス | *merii kurisu mas* |
| ● Happy New Year! | あけましておめでとうございます。 | *akemashite omede toh gozai mas* |
| ● Good luck! | 幸運を祈ります。 | *kohun o inori mas* |
| ● Please keep well. Thank you, same to you. | どうぞお元気で。 ありがとう、あなたも。 | *dohzo ogen ki de arigatoh, anata mo* |
| ● That's... fantastic! terrible! | それは…ですね。 すばらしい ひどい | *sore wa...des ne subarashii hidoi* |
| ● Excuse me./I'm sorry. | すみません。 | *sumimasen* |
| ● What a pity! | 残念ですね。 | *zan nen des ne* |
| ● Hurry! | 急いで。 | *iso ide!* |
| ● Have a safe journey! | 良い旅でありますように。 | *yoii tabi de arimas yoh ni!* |

- **Hello.** (on the phone) — もしもし。 — *moshi moshi*

- **Welcome back.** (said on another's return to your home/office) — おかえりなさい。 — *okaeri nasai*

- **I'm back** (said on your return home). — ただいま。 — *tadaima*

- **Let's enjoy our meal.** — いただきます。 — *itadaki mas*

- **I enjoyed it, thank you.** (polite form) — ごちそうさまでした。 — *gochisoh sama deshita*

- **Cheers!** — 乾杯。 — *kan pai!*

## ✳ business trips

● When exchanging business cards 名刺 (*meishi*) it is essential to present yours held in both hands, and when receiving a card to study it, before placing it on a table, in a holder, but never in a pocket.

● Gift giving is also important. The general cultural rules for corporate gift-giving are that they should be collective rather than personal in nature, wrapped (similarly, literature/documents should be presented in envelopes or document wallets) and either given or received (and not opened in the presence of the giver), rather than simultaneously exchanged.

## ✳ first meeting

### YOU MAY WANT TO SAY...

| | | |
|---|---|---|
| ● Excuse me, I've come for the 10 o'clock meeting. | すみません。10時の会議に来たんですが…。 | *sumimasen. juuji no kaigi ni kitan des ga…* |
| ● I would like to see Mr Yamada, Head of … | …の山田部長にお目にかかりたいんですが…。 | *…no Yamada buchoh ni ome ni kakari tai n des ga…* |
|    sales | 営業 | *eigyoh* |
|    marketing | マーケティング | *mahketingu* |
|    exports | 輸出 | *yushutsu* |
| ● I have an appointment with… | …さんと約束があるんですが…。 | *…san to yakusoku ga arun des ga…* |
| ● How do you do. | はじめまして。 | *hajime mashite* |

- I'm from...
  (company name)
  …の者です。
  *...no mono des*

- My name is...
  …と申します。
  *...to mohshi mas*

- Here is my
  business card.
  私の名刺です。
  *watashi no meishi des*

- I'm pleased to
  meet you.
  どうぞよろしくお願
  いします。
  *dohzo yoroshiku
  onegai shi mas*

## YOU MAY HEAR...

- ようこそ、お越し
  くださいました。
  *yohkoso okoshi
  kudasai mashita*
  Welcome to our
  company.

- お待たせしまし
  た。
  *omatase shimashita*
  Sorry to have kept
  you waiting.

- お茶は、いかがで
  すか。
  *ocha wa ikaga des ka*
  Would you like
  some green tea?

- 日本は初めてです
  か。
  *Nihon wa hajimete
  des ka*
  Is this your first
  time in Japan?

- 日本語がお上手で
  すね。
  *Nihongo ga ojyohzu
  des ne*
  Your Japanese is
  very good.

- とても…ですね。
  暑い
  蒸し暑い
  天気が悪い
  *Totemo ... des ne.
  atsui
  mushiatsui
  tenkiga warui*
  It is very...
  hot
  humid
  wet

- どうぞ、おかけに
  なって下さい。
  *Dohzo okakeni natte
  kudasai*
  Please take a seat.

- 何か他にございま
  すか。
  *Nanika hokani gozai
  maska*
  Anything else?

general conversation

43

## USEFUL WORDS

| | | |
|---|---|---|
| 宣伝 | sen den | advertising |
| 上司 | joh shi | boss |
| 名刺 | mei shi | business card |
| 商談 | shoh dan | business meeting/negotiation |
| 事業計画 | jigyoh keikaku | business plan |
| 会長 | kai choh | Chairman/CEO |
| 会社 | kai sha | company |
| 契約 | kei yaku | contract |
| 契約書にサインをします。 | keiyakusho ni saino shimas | to sign a contract |
| 担当 | tan toh | coordinator/facilitator |
| 社印 | sha in | corporate seal |
| 部長 | bu choh | department head |
| …代理 | …dai ri | deputy… (use as adj) |
| 取締役 | tori shi mari yaku | **Director** (board member) |
| 本部長 | hon bu choo | division head |
| 社員 | sha in | employee |
| マネージャー | ma nei jyah | manager |
| 会議 | kai gi | meeting |
| ハンコ/印鑑 | hanko/in kan | personal seal |
| 有限会社 | yuu gen gai sha | private limited company |
| 社長 | sha choh | President/CEO |

| 公社 | *koh sha* | public company (state owned) |
| 株式会社 | *kabu shiki gai sha* | public limited company |
| 受付 | *uke tsuke* | reception |
| サラリーマン | *sararii man* | 'salaryman', (male officer worker) |
| 売上げ | *uriage* | sales |
| 課長 | *ka choh* | section head |
| 東京証券取引所 | *tohkyoh shohken torihiki jo* | Tokyo Stock Exchange |
| 商社 | *shoh sha* | trading company |
| お得意様 | *otokuisama* | valued customer |

# \* doing business

## YOU MAY WANT TO SAY...

- Ladies and gentlemen.

  みなさま

  *mina sama*

- Here is some information about my company.

  私どもの会社について の説明です。

  *watakushi domo no kaisha ni tsuite no setsumei des*

- Here are the documents for...

  …の資料です

  *...no shiryoh des*

  - our meeting

    会議

    *kaigi*

  - my presentation

    私の発表に関する

    *watashi no happyoh ni kan suru*

| | | |
|---|---|---|
| I'd be grateful if you would read this/that. | これ/それをお読み頂けますでしょうか。 | *kore/sore o oyomi itadake mas de shoh ka* |
| Please let me know if you have any questions. | ご質問がおありでしたら，お願い致します。 | *goshitsu mon ga oari deshita ra, onegai itashi mas* |
| Thank you for your attention; that concludes my presentation. | ご清聴ありがとうございました。これで私の発表を終わらせて頂きます。 | *go seichoh arigatoh gozai mashita. kore de watashi no happyoh o owara sete itadaki mas* |
| May I present you with this gift (from the UK). | （イギリスからの）お土産です。 | *(igirisu kara no) omiyage des* |
| Thank you for coming. | お越しいただき，ありがとうございます。 | *okoshi itadaki, arigatoh gozai mas* |
| I'm sorry, but I must leave soon. | 申し訳ありませんが，もうすぐ失礼させて頂きます。 | *mohshi wake arima senga, mohsugu shitsurei sasete itadaki mas* |
| Shall we have another meeting? | もう一度会議の機会を持ちましょうか。 | *moh ichido kaigi no kikai o mochimashoh ka* |
| See you... | それでは，また…お目にかかります． | *sore dewa, mata... ome ni kakari mas* |
| this evening | 今晩 | *konban* |
| tomorrow | 明日 | *asu* |
| soon | 後ほど | *nochi hodo* |
| in the UK | イギリスで | *igirisu de* |

## YOU MAY HEAR...

| | | |
|---|---|---|
| もう一度言っていただけますか。 | *moh ichido itte itadakemas ka* | **Please can you repeat that.** |
| お食事はいかがですか。 | *oshokuji wa ikaga des ka* | **I'd like to take you out for a meal.** |

# ✱ business entertainment

● Invitations to a drink, an evening of karaoke or a round of golf are offers that cannot really be refused. Whoever extends an invitation expects to pay the bill at the end of the evening. Instead of reciprocating by buying a round of drinks, you can take your turn at being the host on another evening.

## USEFUL WORDS

| | | |
|---|---|---|
| 付き合い | *tsuki ai* | **bonding** |
| 接待 | *settai* | **business entertaining** |
| 隠し芸 | *kakushi gei* | **hidden talent(s)** |
| カラオケ | *kara oke* | **karaoke** |
| オフレコで・非公式で | *ofureko de/hi kohshiki de* | **off-the-record (discussion)** |
| 二次会 | *niji kai* | **second party/venue** |

general conversation

## YOU MAY WANT TO SAY...

- I'd like a...
  …をお願いします
  *...o onegai shimass*

  **draft beer**
  生ビール
  *nama biiru*

  **whisky**
  ウィスキー
  *uisukii*

  …ワイン

- Cheers!
  乾杯!
  *kan pai*

- I don't smoke.
  たばこを吸いません。
  *tabako o sui masen*

- Do you mind if I smoke?
  たばこを吸ってもいいですか?
  *tabako o suttemo ii des ka*

- I'm a vegetarian.
  ベジタリアンです。
  *beji tarian des*

- It's delicious.
  おいしいです。
  *oishii des*

- I'm full.
  お腹が一杯です。
  *onaka ga ippai des*

- Thank you for your hospitality...
  …は, おもてなしありがとうございました。
  *...wa, omote nashi arigatoh gozai mashita*

  **today**
  今日
  *kyoh*

  **tonight**
  今晩
  *konban*

- Would you please call me a taxi?
  タクシーを呼んでいただけますか?
  *takushii o yon de itadake mas ka*

## YOU MAY HEAR...

| 歌がお上手ですね。 | *uta ga ojoh zu des ne* | You sing very well. |
| お箸を使うのが、お上手ですね。 | *o hashi o tsukau noga ojohzu des ne* | You use chopsticks very well. |
| …はいかがですか。 | *...wa ikaga des ka* | Have some more... |
| ビール | *biiru* | beer |
| お酒 | *osake* | sake |

general conversation

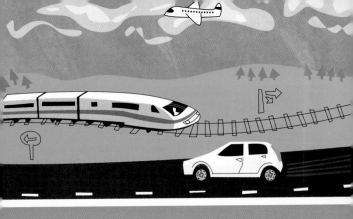

# travel&transport

# ✳ arriving in the country

● Visitors to Japan should have passports valid for at least 6 months, otherwise 'landing permission' will be limited to the duration of the passport's validity. Visitors from the EU may enter and remain in Japan without a visa for up to 180 days. Visas are required for longer stays and can be either 'single entry' or 'multiple re-entry'. You can contact the Japanese embassy in London at www.uk.emb-japan.go.jp/. For useful travel information log on to the website of the Japan National Tourist Organisation (www.jnto.go.jp).

## YOU MAY SEE...

| | | |
|---|---|---|
| 空港 | kuukoh | airport |
| リムジンバス | rimujin basu | airport bus |
| 到着 | tohchaku | arrivals |
| 手荷物引渡し所 | tenimotsu hikiwatashijo | baggage reclaim |
| 税関 | zeikan | customs |
| 出発 | syuppatsu | departures |
| 国内線 | kokunaisen | domestic flights |
| 出口 | deguchi | exit |
| インフォメーション | info meishon | information |
| 国際空港 | kokusai kuukoh | international airport |
| 国際線 | kokusai sen | international flights |
| 入国審査 | nyukoku shinsa | passport control |
| ターミナル | tahmi naru | terminal |
| 日本へようこそ | nihon e yohkoso | welcome to Japan |

- I am here...
  on holiday
  on business
  for a
  sightseeing
  trip

  …来ました。
  休暇で
  仕事で
  観光旅行に

  …kimashita
  kyuuka de
  shigoto de
  kankoh ryokoh ni

- It's for my own personal use.

  それは自分用です。

  sorewa jibun yoh des

- I'm British.

  （私は）イギリス人
  です。

  (watshi wa) igirisu
  jin des

- I'm from Europe.

  （私は）ヨーロッパか
  ら来ました。

  (watashi wa)
  yohroppa kara
  kimashita

- パスポートを拝見
  します。

  pasupohto o haiken
  shimas

  **Your passport
  please.**

- 書類を見せて下さ
  い。

  shorui o misete
  kudasai

  **Your documents
  please.**

- 日本へ来た目的は
  何ですか?

  nihon e kita mokuteki
  wa nan
  des ka

  **What is the purpose
  of your visit?**

- ここにどのくらい
  滞在する予定です
  か?

  kokoni donokurai
  taizai suru yotei
  des ka

  **How long are you
  going to stay here?**

- これからどこへ行
  きますか?

  korekara doko e
  ikimas ka

  **Where are you
  going to now?**

travel and transport

51

| …を開けて下さい | ...o akete kudasai | Please open... |
| このかばん | kono kaban | this bag |
| そのスーツケース | sono suutsu kehsu | that suitcase |
| 荷物を調べさせて頂きます。 | nimotsu o shirabe sasete itadaki mas | We have to search your luggage. |
| 他に荷物はありますか? | hoka ni nimotsu wa arimas ka | Do you have any other luggage? |
| 私と一緒に来てください。 | watashi to isshoni kite kudasai | Come along with me please. |

## \* directions

### YOU MAY SEE...

| 美術館 | bijutsukan | art gallery |
| 大通り | ohdohri | avenue |
| バス停/バス停留所 | basu tei/bas teiryuu syo | bus stop |
| 城 | shiro | castle |
| 教会 | kyohkai | church |
| 自転車道 | jitensha doh | cycle path |
| 病院 | byoh in | hospital |
| 皇居 | koh kyo | the Imperial Palace |
| J R | jeh ahru | Japan Rail/JR |
| 市場 | ichiba | market |
| 博物館 | hakubutsu kan | museum |
| 公園 | kohen | park |
| 交番/警察署 | kohban/keisatsusho | police box/police station |
| 郵便局 | yuubin kyoku | post office |
| 県庁 | kencho | prefectural office |

| 私鉄 | shitetsu | private railway |
| 神社 | jin jya | shrine |
| 駅 | eki | station |
| 通り | tohri | street |
| 寺/寺院 | tera/jiin | temple |
| 地下鉄 | chikatetsu | underground |

## YOU MAY WANT TO SAY...

- Excuse me, please. / すみません。 / sumimasen

- Where is/are... / …はどこにありますか / ...wa doko ni arimas ka?

  the tourist centre? / ツーリストセンター/観光案内所 / tuurisuto sentah/ kankoh an naisho

  the station? / 駅 / eki
  the cash point? / ATM / eh tii emu
  the toilets? / トイレ / toire

- Where is/are the nearest... ? / いちばん近い… はどこですか? / ichiban chikai ... wa doko des ka

- How do we get to... / …にはどうやって行きますか? / ...niwa doh yatte iki mas ka

  the airport? / 空港 / kuukoh
  the beach? / 海岸 / kaigan

- I'm/We're lost. / (私/私たちは)道に迷ってしまいました。 / (watashi/watashi tachi wa) michi ni mayotte shimai mashita

- Is this the right way to... ? / …へ行くのはこの道でいいんですか? / ...e iku nowa kono michi de ii n des ka

travel and transport

53

- Can you show me on the map, please? | 地図で教えてください。 | *chizu de oshiete kudasai*
- Is it far? | 遠いですか? | *tohi des ka*
- Is there ... near here | この近くに … はありますか? | *kono chikaku ni ... wa ari mas ka*
  - a bank? | 銀行 | *gin koh*

## YOU MAY HEAR...

- 私たちはここにいます。 | *watashi tachi wa koko ni imas* | We are here.
- こちらです。 | *kochira des* | This way.
- あちらです。 | *achira des* | That way.
- まっすぐです。 | *massugu des* | Straight on.
- …に曲がって下さい | *...ni magatte kudasai* | Turn...
  - 右 | *migi* | right
  - 左 | *hidari* | left
- …行って下さい | *...itte kudasai* | Go on...
  - この道の突き当たりまで | *kono michi no tsuki atari made* | to the end of the street
  - 次の信号まで | *tsugi no shin goh made* | to the traffic lights
- 最初の角を … に曲がって下さい | *saisho no kado o ... ni magatte kudasai* | Take the first on the...
  - 右 | *migi* | right
  - 左 | *hidari* | left

| | | |
|---|---|---|
| …にあります | …ni arimas | It's… |
| …の前 | …no mae | in front of… |
| 向かい側 | mukaigawa | opposite |
| 後ろ | ushiro | behind |
| …の近くに | …no chikaku ni | close to… |
| …の隣に | …no tonari ni | next to… |
| とても近い/遠いです。 | totemo chikai/tohi des | It's very near/far away. |
| 五分の所にあります。 | gofun no tokoro ni ari mas | It's five minutes away. |
| …番のバスに乗らなければなりません。 | …ban no basu ni nora nakereba narima sen | You have to take bus number… |

## ✱ information and tickets

(see **telling the time**, page 20)

● Some signage, particularly in major rail and underground stations and airports is in English, though less commonly found in bus/coach stations and ferry ports.

● Tickets are available from station vending machines 自動切符売り場 *(jidoh kippu uriba)*, ticket offices, travel agencies, Tourist Information Centres and online. The availability of 'Fare Adjustment Offices' 精算所 *(seisanjo)* means that you don't have to worry about purchasing the correct ticket, any excess due can easily be 'adjusted' at your destination.

travel and transport

### YOU MAY WANT TO SAY...

| | | |
|---|---|---|
| Is there a train/bus/boat to... ? | …行きの電車/バス/船はありますか？ | ...iki no densha/basu/fune wa arimas ka |
| What time is the... | …は何時ですか？ | ... wa nan ji des ka |
| next train ? | 次の電車 | tsugi no densha |
| last train? | 終電 | shuuden |
| first bus ? | 始発のバス | shihatsu no basu |
| To Kyoto | 京都行き | kyoto iki |
| Do trains go often? | 電車は頻繁に出ますか？ | densha wa hinpan ni demas ka |
| What time does it arrive in...? | …に何時に着きますか？ | ...ni nanji ni tsuki mas ka |
| Do I have to change? | 乗り換えが必要ですか？ | norikae ga hitsuyoh des ka |
| Which platform for ...? | …行きは何番線ですか？ | ...iki wa nan ban sen des ka |
| Which bus stop for ...? | …行きのバス停はどこですか？ | ...iki no basu teh wa doko des ka |
| Where can I buy a ticket? | 切符はどこで買えますか？ | Kippu wa doko de kae mas ka |
| One/two tickets to ... please. | …まで，一枚/二枚お願いします。 | ...made, ichimai/nimai onegai shimas |
| single | 片道 | kata michi |
| return | 往復 | oh fuku |
| For... | …行き | ...iki |
| two adults | 大人二枚 | otona nimai |
| three children | 子供三枚 | kodomo san mai |
| a car | 車一台 | kuruma ichi dai |

| | | |
|---|---|---|
| ● I want to reserve... | …を予約したいんですが? | ...o yoyaku shitai n des ga |
| a seat/s | 席 | seki |
| a cabin/s | 船室 | sen shitsu |
| ● Is there a supplement? | 追加料金が掛かりますか? | tsuika ryohkin ga kakari mas ka |
| ● Is there a discount for... | …はありますか? | ...wa arimas ka |
| students? | 学生割引 | gakusei waribiki |
| senior citizens? | シニアの割引 | shinia no waribiki |

## YOU MAY HEAR...

| | | |
|---|---|---|
| ● …時出発です | ...ji shuppatsu des | It leaves at... |
| ● …時着です | ...ji chaku des | It arrives at... |
| ● 十分ごとに出ます。 | juppun goto ni demas | They go every ten minutes. |
| ● 乗り換えが必要です。 | norikae ga hitsuyoh des | You have to change. |
| ● 四番線です。 | yon ban sen des | It's platform four. |
| ● 切符は … 買えます | kippu wa ... kae mas | You can buy a ticket... |
| 駅で | eki de | at the station |
| バスの中で | basu no naka de | on the bus |
| 電車の中で | densha no naka de | on the train |
| 船の中で | fune no naka de | on the boat |
| ● バス/電車の中で払えます | basu/densha no naka de harae mas | You can pay on the bus/train. |
| ● 運転手にお支払い下さい。 | unten shu ni oshi harai kuda sai | You can pay the driver. |

travel and transport

57

| いつ … ですか? | itsu … des ka | When do you want to... |
|---|---|---|
| ご出発 | goshuppatsu | travel? |
| お帰り | oka eri | come back? |
| 片道ですか，往復ですか? | kata michi des ka, oh fuku des ka | Single or return? |
| 喫煙席ですか，禁煙席ですか? | kitsuen seki des ka, kinen seki des ka | Smoking or non-smoking? |
| …の追加料金が掛かります。 | …no tsuika ryohkin ga kakari mas | There's a supplement of... |

## ✳ trains

(see **information and tickets**, page 55)

As well as a variety of local and inter-city trains, Japan has the *shinkansen* (新幹線), the 'bullet' trains (*shinkansen* actually means 'new express line'). They have their own tracks and platforms. *Kodama* services stop at all *shinkansen* stations, *Hikari* services stop at fewer and *Nozomi shinkansen*, the fastest in the fleet, stop only at the most important stations. *Shinkansen* fares vary according to *Kodama*, *Hikari* and *Nozomi* services. グリーン券 *(greenken)*, is charged for reserved seats in first class carriages, known as 'Green Cars'.

Japan Rail Passes, available only outside Japan, enable you to travel (with reserved seats included) on trains and JR buses and ferries, for periods of 7, 14 or 21 days (consecutively, from first validation).

travel and transport

## YOU MAY SEE...

| 到着 | tohchaku | arrivals |
|---|---|---|
| 新幹線 | shin kan sen | 'bullet train' |
| コインロッカー | koin rokkah | coin lockers |
| 行き先 | ikisaki | destination |
| 食堂車 | shoku doh sha | dining car |
| 精算機 | seisanki | fare adjustment machine |
| グリーン車 | guriin sha | first class ('green cars') |
| 情報/インフォメーション | joh hoh/info mei shon | information |
| 手荷物預り所 | tenimotsu azukari sho | left luggage |
| 各駅停車 | kaku eki teisha | local train |
| 紛失物取扱所 | fu n shitsu butsu toriatsukai jo | lost property |
| 自由席 | jiyuu seki | non-reserved seats |
| 番線/ホーム | ban sen/hohmu | platform |
| スイカ(Suica) | suika | pre-paid card |
| 指定席 | shitei seki | reserved seats |
| 予約/指定 | yoyaku/shiteh | reservations |
| シルバーシート | sirubah shiito | 'silver seat' (elderly/handicapped/pregnant women) |
| 寝台車 | shindai sha | sleeping-car |
| 特急電車 | tokkyuu densha | super-express train |
| 切符売り場 | kippu uriba | ticket office |
| 切符 | kippu | tickets |
| トイレ/お手洗い | toire/otearai | toilets |
| 乗り場へ | noriba e | to the platforms |
| 下り | kudari | trains leaving Tokyo |
| 上り | nobori | trains to Tokyo |

travel and transport

- I'd like a single/
  return ticket to
  Kyoto please.

  京都まで片道/往復の
  切符を一枚，お願い
  します。

  kyoto made kata
  michi/oh fuku no
  kippu o ichi mai
  onegai shimas

- Are there lifts to
  the platform?

  プラットホームへの
  エレベーターはあり
  ますか

  puratto hohmu eno
  erebehtah wa ari
  mas ka

- Does this train go
  to Shibuya?

  この電車は渋谷に行
  きますか？

  kono den sha wa
  shibuya ni iki mas ka

- Excuse me, I've
  reserved...

     that seat.

  すみませんが、…の
  予約があるんです
  が…その席.
     その席

  sumimasen ga, ... no
  yoyaku ga arun des
  ga...
     sono seki

- Is this seat taken?

  この席にだれかいま
  すか？

  kono seki ni dare ka
  imas ka

- May I...
     open the
        window?
     smoke?

  …いいですか？
     窓を開けても

     タバコを吸っても

  ...ii des ka
     mado o ake temo

     tabako o sutte mo

- Where are we?

  ここはどこですか？

  koko wa doko des ka

- How long does
  the train stop
  here?

  電車はここにどのく
  らい停車しますか？

  densha wa koko ni
  dono kurai teisha
  shimas ka

- Can you tell me
  when we get to
  Narita?

  何時に成田に着くか
  教えてください？

  nanji ni Narita ni
  tsuku ka oshi ete
  kudasai

# ✱ buses and coaches

(see **information and tickets**, page 55)

● Destinations are displayed in *kanji* on the front and side, stops are announced in Japanese, and changes are often required, making it vital to obtain a transfer ticket *(noritsugi johshaken)*. Coaches, including all-night coaches, run between major cities and to ski and tourist resorts.

## YOU MAY SEE...

| | | |
|---|---|---|
| バス停留所/ターミナル | *basu tei ryuu jo/tah minaru* | bus station/terminal |
| バス停 | *basu tei* | bus stop |
| バス | *basu* | coach |
| 非常口 | *hijoh guchi* | emergency exit |
| 入口/入り口 | *iriguchi* | entrance |
| 長距離バス | *choh kyori basu* | long-distance coach |
| 禁煙 | *kinen* | no smoking |

## YOU MAY WANT TO SAY...

● Where does the bus to the town centre leave from?

市内行きのバスはどこから出ますか？

*shinai iki no basu wa doko kara demas ka*

● Does the bus to the airport leave from here?

空港へのバスはここから出ますか？

*kuukoh eno basu wa koko kara demas ka*

**travel and transport**

61

## buses and coaches

- **What number is it?** それは何番ですか？ *sore wa nan ban des ka*

- **Does this bus go to...** このバスは … へ行きますか？ *kono basu wa ... e iki mas ka*
  - the beach? 海 *umi*
  - the station? 駅 *eki*

- **Can you tell me where to get off, please?** どこで降りたらいいか教えて下さい？ *doko de ori tara ii ka oshi ete kudasai*

- **Excuse me, I'm getting off here.** すみません。ここで降ります。 *sumimasen. koko de ori mas*

- **The next stop, please.** 次のバス停で，お願いします。 *tsugi no basu teh de, onegai shimas*

- **Can you open the doors, please?** ドアを開けてください。 *doa o akete kudasai*

### YOU MAY HEAR...

市内行きのバスはここから出ます。 *shinai iki no basu wa koko kara demas*
The bus to the town centre leaves from here.

五十七番のバスが駅へ行きます。 *gojuu nana ban no basu ga eki e iki mas*
The number 57 goes to the station.

次の停留所で降りてください。 *tsugi no teh ryuu jo de orite kudasai*
You must get off at the next stop.

（お客さんは）乗り越してしまいました。 *(okyaku san wa) nori koshite shimai mashita*
You've missed the stop.

# ✻ underground

(see **information and tickets**, page 55)

● All of Japan's nine largest cities have underground systems 地下鉄 *(chikatetsu)*. In Tokyo there are a variety of pre-paid passes which are cheaper and more convenient than buying a ticket for each journey.

## YOU MAY SEE...

| | | |
|---|---|---|
| 入口／入り口 | *iriguchi* | **entrance** |
| 出口 | *deguchi* | **exit** |
| 一番線/1番線 | *ichibansen* | **platform 1** |
| 千代田線 | *chiyoda sen* | **Chiyoda line** |
| 丸の内線 | *marunouchi sen* | **Marunouchi line** |

## YOU MAY WANT TO SAY...

● I'd like a day ticket please.
一日券をお願いします。
*ichi nichi ken o onegai shimas*

● Do you have a map of the underground?
地下鉄の地図がありますか？
*chika tetsu no chizu ga arimas ka*

● Which line is it for the airport?
空港に行くのは何線ですか？
*kuu koh ni iku nowa nani sen des ka*

● Which stop is it for... ?
…へ行くにはどの駅で降りますか？
*...e iku niwa dono eki de ori mas ka*

● Is this the right stop for... ?
…へはここでいいんですか？
*...e wa kokode ii n des ka*

● Does this train go to...?
この電車は … へ行きますか？
*kono densha wa ... e iki mas ka*

## YOU MAY HEAR...

| | | |
|---|---|---|
| ２番線です。 | *niban sen des* | It's platform number two. |
| 次の駅です。 | *tsugi no eki des* | It's the next stop. |
| 一つ前の駅でした。 | *hitotsu mae no eki deshita* | It was the last stop. |

# ✳ boats and ferries

(see **information and tickets**, page 55)

● In addition to ferry and jet foil services between Kyushu, western Honshu and Korea, there are ferry services between all four main islands, as well as boat services between Tokyo and Hokkaido and as far south as Okinawa.

## YOU MAY SEE...

| | | |
|---|---|---|
| 船/ボート | *fune/bohto* | boats |
| 船室 | *sen shitsu* | cabins |
| クルーズ/船旅 | *kuruuzu/funatabi* | cruises |
| フェリー/連絡船 | *ferii/renraku sen* | ferry |
| 救命ボート | *kyuu mei bohto* | lifeboat |
| 救命胴衣 | *kyuu mei dohi* | life jacket |
| 桟橋/埠頭 | *senbashi/futoh* | pier |
| 港 | *minato* | port |

- I'd like a return ticket to... please

  …への往復切符をお願いします。

  *...e no ohfuku kippu o onegai shimas*

- Is there a ferry to... today?

  今日は … 行きのフェリーがありますか?

  *kyoh wa ... iki no ferii ga ari mas ka*

- Are there any boat trips?

  川下りの船は出ますか

  *kawa kudari no fune wa demas ka*

- How long is the cruise?

  クルーズの時間はどのくらいですか?

  *kuruuzu no jikan wa dono kurai des ka*

- Is there wheelchair access?

  車椅子でも乗れますか?

  *kuruma isu demo nore mas ka*

- What is the sea like today?

  今日の海の状態はどうですか?

  *kyoh no umi no johtai wa doh des ka*

- Is it possible to go out on deck?

  デッキに出ることができますか?

  *dekki ni deru koto ga deki mas ka*

- 船は … 出ます
  火曜日と金曜日に
  一日おきに

  *fune wa ... demas
  kayoh bi to kin yohbi ni
  ichi nichi oki ni*

  Boats go on...
  Tuesdays and Fridays
  every other day

- 海は…
  静かです
  波があります

  *umi wa ...
  shizuka des
  nami ga arimas*

  The sea is...
  calm
  choppy

travel and transport

# ✳ air travel

(see **information and tickets**, page 55)

| | | |
|---|---|---|
| 空港 | *kuukoh* | airport |
| 到着 | *tohchaku* | arrivals |
| 搭乗 | *tohjoh* | boarding |
| 搭乗ゲート | *tohjoh geito* | boarding gate |
| 両替 | *ryoh gae* | bureau de change |
| チェックイン | *chekku in* | check-in |
| 税関 | *zeikan* | customs |
| 遅れ/遅延 | *okure/chien* | delay |
| 出発ロビー | *shuppatsu robii* | departure lounge |
| 出発 | *shuppatsu* | departures |
| 国際線出発 | *kokusai sen shuppatsu* | international departures |
| 手荷物引渡し所 | *tenimotsu hikiwatashi jo* | luggage reclaim |
| 入国審査 | *nyuu koku shinsa* | passport control |
| 警備 | *keibi* | security |

## YOU MAY WANT TO SAY...

- **I'd like a return ticket to... please.**
  …行きの往復切符をお願いします。
  *...iki no oh fuku kippu o onegai shimas*

- **I want to change/cancel my ticket.**
  チケットの変更/キャンセルをしたいんですが。
  *chiketto no henkoh/kyan seru o shitain des ga*

- **What time do I/we have to check in?**
  何時にチェックインしければなりませんか?
  *nan ji ni chekkuin shinakereba narimasen ka*

- **Is there a delay?** 　遅れているのですか？　*okurete iruno des ka*

- **Which gate is it?** 　どのゲートですか？　*dono geito des ka*

- **Have you got a wheelchair?** 　車椅子がありますか？　*kuruma isu ga ari mas ka*

- **My luggage hasn't arrived.** 　私の荷物が届いていません。　*watashi no nimotsu ga todo ite imasen*

- **Is there a bus/ train to the centre of town?** 　市内行きのバス/電車がありますか？　*shinai iki no basu/ densha ga ari mas ka*

## WORDS TO LISTEN OUT FOR...

| 呼び出し | *yobidashi* | call |
| キャンセル | *kyanseru* | cancelled |
| 遅れ | *okure* | delay |
| フライト | *furaito* | flight |
| ゲート | *geito* | gate |
| 最終案内 | *saishu annai* | last call |

## ✳ taxis

(see **directions**, page 52)

- The driver controls the near-side passenger door with an automatic release; passengers wait for this door to open, both on entering and leaving. It is advisable to have a street map or faxed map, as well as the address written in *kanji* to show the driver on entry (many business cards in Japan have maps on their reverse sides for this purpose). Tipping is not expected.

## YOU MAY WANT TO SAY...

| | | |
|---|---|---|
| Is there a taxi rank round here? | この近くにタクシー乗り場がありますか? | *konochikaku ni takushii noriba ga arimas ka* |
| Can you order me a taxi...<br>immediately<br>for tomorrow<br>at nine o'clock | …タクシーをお願いします<br>すぐに<br>明日の9時に | *...takushii o onegai shimas*<br>*sugu ni*<br>*asu no kuji ni* |
| To this address, please. | この住所までお願いします。 | *kono juusho made onegai shimas* |
| How much will it cost? | 料金はいくらになりますか? | *ryohkin wa ikura ni nari mas ka* |
| How far is it from here? | ここからどのくらいですか? | *koko kara dono kurai des ka* |
| I'm in a hurry. | 急いでいます。 | *isoide imas* |
| Stop here, please. | ここで停めて下さい。 | *kokode tomete kudasai* |
| Can you wait for me, please? | ここで待ってもらえますか? | *kokode matte morae mas ka* |
| I think there's a mistake. | 間違いだと思うんですが…。 | *machigai dato omou n des ga...* |
| Can you give me a receipt, please? | レシートを下さい? | *reshiito o kudasai* |

## YOU MAY HEAR...

| | | |
|---|---|---|
| どちらまでですか？ | dochira made des ka | Where would you like to go? |
| 十キロ先です。 | jukkiro saki des | It's ten kilometres away. |
| だいたい千五百円ぐらいになります。 | daitai sen gohyaku en gurai ni nari mas | It'll cost about ¥1,500. |
| 千八百円になります。 | sen happyaku en ni nari mas | That's ¥1,800. |
| 夜間の追加料金が掛かります。 | yakan no tsuika ryohkin ga kakari mas | There's a supplement for late-night services. |
| どちらからですか？ | dochira kara des ka | Where are you from? |

## ✳ hiring cars and bicycles

### YOU MAY WANT TO SAY...

| | | |
|---|---|---|
| I'd like to hire... | …借りたいんですが。 | ...kari tai n des ga |
| two bicycles | 自転車を二台 | jitensha o nidai |
| a small car | 小型車を一台 | kogata sha o ichi dai |
| a car with a satellite navigation system | カーナビ付きの車を一台 | kah nabi tsuki no kuruma o ichi dai |
| For one hour. | 一時間。 | ichi jikan |

# hiring cars and bicycles

| | | |
|---|---|---|
| **For one day.** | 一日。 | *ichi nichi* |
| **For a week.** | 一週間。 | *isshuu kan* |
| **For two weeks.** | 二週間。 | *ni shuu kan* |
| **Until...** | …まで | *...made* |
| Friday | 金曜日 | *kin yohbi* |
| the 17th | 八月十七日 | *hachi gatsu juu* |
| August | | *shichi nichi* |
| **How much is it...** | …いくらですか | *...ikura des ka?* |
| per day? | 一日 | *ichi nichi* |
| per week? | 一週間 | *isshuu kan* |
| **Is insurance included?** | 保険は含まれていますか? | *hoken wa fukumarete imas ka* |
| **My partner wants to drive too.** | 私の連れも運転したいんですが。 | *watashi no tsure mo unten shitai n des ga* |
| **Is the full payment due now or when I return the car?** | 支払いは今ですか、それとも車を返す時ですか? | *shiharai wa ima des ka, sore tomo kuruma o kaesu toki des ka* |
| **Do you take...** | …は使えますか? | *...wa tsukae mas ka* |
| credit cards? | クレジットカード | *Kurejitto kahdo* |
| travellers' cheques? | トラベラーズチェック | *Toraberahzu chekku* |
| **Can I leave the car...** | …車を乗り捨てできますか? | *...kuruma o nori sute deki mas ka* |
| at the airport? | 空港で | *kuukoh de* |
| in the town centre? | 市内で | *shinai de* |
| **How much is it for ...** | …いくらですか? | *...ikura des ka* |
| one hour? | 一時間 | *ichi jikan* |
| six hours? | 六時間 | *roku jikan* |

| | | |
|---|---|---|
| ● **Can you put the saddle up/down, please?** | サドルを上げて/下げてください。 | *sadoru o agete/ sagete kuda sai* |

## YOU MAY HEAR...

| | | |
|---|---|---|
| ● どんなタイプの車/自転車がよろしいですか? | *don na taipu no kuruma/jitensha ga yoroshii des ka* | **What kind of car/bicycle do you want?** |
| ● いつからいつまでですか? | *itsu kara itsu made des ka* | **For how long?** |
| ● 運転免許証を見せて下さい。 | *unten menkyosho o misete kudasai* | **Your driving licence/s, please** |
| ● 追加の保険は必要ですか? | *tsuika no hoken wa hitsuyoh des ka* | **Do you want extra insurance?** |
| ● クレジットカードはありますか? | *kurejitto kahdo wa ari mas ka* | **Have you got a credit card?** |
| ● 満タンにして車をお返し下さい。 | *mantan ni shite kuruma o okaeshi kudasai* | **Please return the car with a full tank.** |
| ● 六時までに車/自転車をお返し下さい。 | *rokuji made ni kuruma/jitensha o okaeshi kudasai* | **Please return the car/bicycle before six o'clock.** |

# ✳ driving

(see **directions**, page 52)

● The Japanese drive on the left.

● Japanese cars use レギュラー (*regyurah*) unleaded petrol. European makes take ハイオク (*haioku*) high octane.

## YOU MAY SEE...

| | | |
|---|---|---|
| 駐車場 | *chuusha jyoh* | car park |
| バス専用 | *basu senyoh* | buses only |
| 迂回路 | *ukairo* | diversion |
| ETC | *ii tii shii* | electronic toll collection |
| 緊急電話 | *kinkyuu denwa* | emergency telephone |
| 出口 | *deguchi* | exit |
| 高速道路 | *kohsoku dohro* | expressway |
| 一時停止/前方優先道路 | *ichiji teishi/zenpoh yuusen dohro* | give way |
| 交差点 | *kohsa ten* | level crossing |
| 高速道路 | *kohsoku dohro* | motorway |
| 追越し禁止 | *oikoshi kinshi* | no overtaking |
| 駐車禁止 | *chuusha kinshi* | no parking |
| 停車禁止 | *teisha kinshi* | no stopping |
| 行き止まり | *iki domari* | no through road |
| 一方通行 | *ippoh tsuukoh* | one-way |
| ガソリン | *gasorin* | petrol |

| ハイオク | hai oku | (premium; high-octane) |
| レギュラー | regyurah | (unleaded) petrol |
| ガソリンスタンド | gasorin sutando | petrol station |
| セルフ | serufu | 'self-service' petrol station |
| 学校 | gakkoh | school |
| サービスエリア | sahbisu eria | services on motorway |
| 徐行 | jokoh | slow |
| 止まれ | tomare | stop |
| 料金所 | ryohkin jo | toll |

## YOU MAY WANT TO SAY...

| **Where is the nearest petrol station?** | いちばん近いガソリンスタンドはどこですか? | *ichiban chikai gasorin sutando wa doko des ka* |
| **Fill it up with...** | …で満タンにして下さい。 | *...de man tan ni shite kudasai* |
| unleaded | レギュラー | *regyurah* |
| **¥2,000 worth of unleaded, please.** | レギュラーを2000円分お願いします。 | *regyurah o nisen en bun onegai shimas* |
| **20 litres of leaded, please.** | ハイオクを20リットルお願いします。 | *hai oku o nijuu rittoru onegai shimas* |
| **Can you check the tyre pressure, please?** | タイヤの空気圧を調べてください。 | *taiya no kuuki atsu o shira bete kudasai* |
| **Please wash the car.** | 洗車をお願いします。 | *sen sha o onegai shimas* |

travel and transport

73

## YOU MAY HEAR...

| | | |
|---|---|---|
| いらっしゃいませ。 | *irasshai mase* | What would you like? |
| どのくらい必要ですか? | *dono kurai hitsuyoh des ka* | How much do you want? |
| 窓を洗ってもよろしいですか? | *mado o arattemo yoroshii des ka* | Do you want me to clean the windscreen and windows? |

## * mechanical problems

### YOU MAY WANT TO SAY...

| | | |
|---|---|---|
| My car has broken down. | 車が故障してしまいました。 | *Kuruma ga koshoh shite shimai mashita* |
| I've run out of petrol. | ガソリンを切らしてしまいました。 | *gasorin o kirashite shimai mashita* |
| I have a puncture. | パンクしてしまいました。 | *pan ku shite shimai mashita* |
| Do you do repairs? | 修理できますか? | *shuuri dekimas ka* |
| I don't know what's wrong. | どこが悪いかわかりません。 | *doko ga warui ka wakari masen* |
| The ... doesn't work. | …が動きません。 | *...ga ugoki masen* |
| Is it serious? | 簡単には直りませんか? | *kan tan niwa naori masen ka* |
| Can you repair it today? | 今日中に直してもらえますか? | *kyoh juu ni naoshite morae mas ka* |

travel and transport

| | | |
|---|---|---|
| ● When will it be ready? | いつ出来ますか? | *itsu deki mas ka* |
| ● How much will it cost? | いくらかぐらいかかりますか? | *ikura gurai kakari mas ka* |

### YOU MAY HEAR...

| | | |
|---|---|---|
| ● どこが悪いのですか? | *doko ga warui no des ka* | What's wrong with it? |
| ● パーツがありません。 | *pahtsu ga ari masen* | I don't have the necessary parts. |
| ● …出来ます 一時間で 月曜日に | *...deki mas ichi jikan de getsu yohbi ni* | It'll be ready... in an hour on Monday |

## ✳ car parts

### YOU MAY WANT TO SAY...

| | | |
|---|---|---|
| accelerator | アクセル | *akuseru* |
| back tyre | 後輪 | *kohrin* |
| battery | バッテリー | *batterii* |
| bonnet | ボンネット | *bon netto* |
| bumper | バンパー | *banpah* |
| child seat | チャイルドシート | *chairudo shiito* |
| engine | エンジン | *enjin* |
| exhaust pipe | 排気管 | *haiki kan* |
| fanbelt | ファンベルト | *fan beruto* |
| front tyre | 前輪 | *zenrin* |
| fuel gauge | 燃料計 | *nenryoh kei* |

travel and transport

75

| gears | ギア | *gia* |
| headlights | ヘッドライト | *heddo raito* |
| ignition | イグニッション | *igunisshon* |
| indicator | 方向指示器 | *hoh koh shijiki* |
| radiator | ラジエーター | *raji ehtah* |
| rear lights | テールランプ | *tehru ranpu* |
| reversing lights | バックライト | *bakku raito* |
| side lights | サイドランプ | *saido ranpu* |
| starter motor | スターター | *sutah tah* |
| steering wheel | ハンドル | *handoru* |
| windscreen | フロントガラス | *furonto garasu* |
| windscreen wiper | ワイパー | *waipah* |

## \* bicycle parts

**YOU MAY WANT TO SAY...**

| back light | バックライト | *bakku raito* |
| chain | チェーン | *cheehn* |
| frame | フレーム | *fureimu* |
| front light | フロントライト | *furonto raito* |
| gears | ギア | *gia* |
| handlebars | ハンドル | *handoru* |
| inner tube | チューブ | *chuubu* |
| pump | ポンプ | *ponpu* |
| saddle | サドル | *sadoru* |
| tyre | タイヤ | *taiya* |
| valve | バルブ | *barubu* |
| wheel | 車輪 | *sharin* |

# accommodation

## ✳ accommodation

 In many Japanese hotels there is a choice of room: western-style 洋室 (*yohshitsu*), or Japanese-style 和室 (*washitsu*). Japanese rooms have traditional woven flooring 畳 (*tatami*).

● Traditional Japanese inns 旅館 (*ryokan*), offer *washitsu* and serve exclusively Japanese cuisine, usually in your room. Guests are given use of 浴衣 *yukata* (a cotton kimono), and Japanese sandals (草履 soft *zohri*, or wooden 下駄 *geta*). Rooms have their own bathrooms but also communal (single-sex) baths お風呂 (*ofuro*). The Japanese use the American convention when referring to floors, e.g. first floor is UK ground floor etc.

### YOU MAY SEE...

| | | |
|---|---|---|
| 地下 | chika | basement |
| 浴室 | yokushitsu | bathroom |
| 朝食 | choh shoku | breakfast |
| 宿坊 | shukuboh | Buddhist temple lodge |
| ビジネスホテル | bijinesu hoteru | business hotel |
| カプセルホテル | kapuseru hoteru | capsule hotel |
| 食堂/レストラン | shokudoh/resutoran | dining room |
| 飲料水 | inryoh sui | drinking water |
| 非常口 | hijoh guchi | emergency exit |
| 出口 | deguchi | exit |
| ガレージ | gareiji | garage |

| 一階 | ikkai | ground floor |
|------|-------|--------------|
| ホテル | hoteru | hotel |
| 旅館 | ryokan | inn |
| 民宿 | minshuku | Japanese style bed and breakfast |
| 洗濯室 | sentaku shitsu | laundry |
| ロビー | robii | lobby |
| 露天風呂 | roten buro | outdoor bath (hot spring) |
| 下履き（下駄） | shita baki (geta) | outdoor footwear |
| 駐車場 | chuusha joh | parking |
| 呼び鈴を鳴らして下さい | yobirin o narashite kudasai | please ring the bell |
| 国民宿舎 | kokumin shukusha | 'People's lodge' |
| フロント／受付 | furonto/uketsuke | reception |
| レストラン | resutoran | restaurant |
| シャワー | shawah | showers |
| トイレ（男性用） | toire (dansei yoh) | toilets (Male) |
| トイレ（女性用） | toire (josei yoh) | toilets (Female) |
| 洋式トイレ | yohshiki toire | Western-style toilets |

## ✱ booking in advance

(see **telephones**, page 163; **national holidays**, page 27)

● The Japanese are accustomed to booking accommodation in advance, and this is vital if you are visiting Japan during national holiday periods, particularly 'Golden Week' (*gohruden uiiku*).

## booking in advance

- **Do you have a ...** …はありますか? ...wa arimas ka
    - **single?** シングルの部屋 singuru no heya
    - **double?** ダブルの部屋 daburu no heya
    - **family room?** 家族部屋 kazoku beya
    - **twin-bedded room?** ツインの部屋 tsuin no heya

- **Do you have...** …はありますか? ...wa arimas ka
    - **rooms?** 部屋 heya
    - **space for a tent?** テントを張る場所 tento o haru basho

- **For... one night** 一泊 ippaku
    - **two nights** 二泊 nihaku
    - **a week** 一週間 isshuukan

- **from... to...** …から…まで ...kara ...ma de

- **with...** …付き ...tsuki
    - **bath** （お）風呂 (o) furo
    - **shower** シャワー shawah

- **It's a two-person tent.** 二人用のテントです。 futari yoh no tento des

- **How much is it...** いくらですか? ikura des ka
    - **per night?** 一泊 ippaku
    - **per week?** 一週間 isshuukan

- **Is breakfast included?** 朝食付きですか? chohshoku tsuki des ka

- **Is there...** …はありますか? ...wa arimas ka
    - **a reduction for children?** 子供の割引き kodomo no waribiki
    - **wheelchair access?** 車椅子用通路 kuruma isu yoh tsuuro

accommodation

| | | |
|---|---|---|
| • Do you have... anything cheaper? | …はありますか？ もっと安い部屋 | ...wa arimas ka motto yasui heya |
| • Can I pay by... credit card? travellers' cheques? | …で支払えますか？ クレジットカード トラベラーズチェ ック | ...de shiharae mas ka kurejitto kahdo toraberahzu chekku |
| • Can I book online? | インターネットで予 約できますか？ | intah netto de yoyaku deki mas ka |
| • What's your website address? | ホームページのア ドレスを教えて下 さい。 | hohmu peiji no adoresu o oshiete kudasai |
| • Could you recommend anywhere else? | 他にどこかお勧めの 場所がありますか。 | hoka ni dokoka osnsume no basho ga arimas ka? |

## YOU MAY HEAR...

| | | |
|---|---|---|
| • いらっしゃいま せ。 | irasshai mase | May I help you? |
| • いつお越しになり ますか。 | itsu okoshi ni narimas ka? | When do you want to come? |
| • 何泊なさいます か。 | nan paku nasai mas ka? | For how many nights? |
| • 何名様ですか。 | nan mei sama des ka? | For how many people? |
| • シングルとダブル のどちらがよろし いですか。 | shinguru to daburu no dochira ga yoroshii des ka? | Single or double room? |

accommodation

81

| | | |
|---|---|---|
| ダブルのベッドが よろしいですか。 | daburu no beddo ga yoroshii des ka? | Do you want a double bed? |
| お名前をお願いし ます。 | onamae o onegai shimas | What's your name, please? |
| クレジットカード をお持ちですか。 | kurejitto kahdo o omochi des ka? | Do you have a credit card? |
| 朝食付きで一泊一 万円になります。 | choh shoku tsuki de ippaku ichiman en ni narimas | It's ¥10,000 per night, including breakfast. |
| 申し訳ありません が，満室です。 | mohshi wake arimasenga, manshitsu des | I'm sorry, we're full. |

## ✳ checking in

### YOU MAY WANT TO SAY...

| | | |
|---|---|---|
| I have a reservation for... tonight two nights a week | …の予約をしてあ ります 今晩 二泊 一週間 | ...no yoyaku o shite arimas konban nihaku isshuukan |
| It's in the name of... | …の名前で予約して います。 | ...no namae de yoyaku shite imas |
| Here's my passport. | 私のパスポートで す。 | watashi no pasupohto des |
| I'm paying by credit card. | クレジットカードで 支払います。 | kurejitto kahdo de shiharai mas |

accommodation

82

## YOU MAY HEAR...

| | | |
|---|---|---|
| お部屋/場所を予約をしていらっしゃいますか? | oheya/basho o yoyaku shite irrashaimas ka | Have you reserved a room/space? |
| お名前をお願いします。 | onamae o onegai shimas | What's your name? |
| パスポートを見せて頂けますか? | pasupohto o misete itadake mas ka | Can I have your passport, please? |
| お支払いはどのようになさいますか? | oshiharai wa dono yohni nasai mas ka | How would you like to pay? |
| クレジットカードのコピーをとらせて下さい? | kurejitto kahdo no kopii o torasete kudasai | Can I take a copy of your credit card? |

## REGISTRATION CARD INFORMATION

| | |
|---|---|
| 姓 | surname |
| 名 | first name |
| 郵便番号 | postcode |
| 本国の住所/通り/番号 | home address/street/number |
| 国籍 | nationality |
| 職業 | occupation |
| 生年月日 | date of birth |
| 出生地 | place of birth |
| パスポート番号 | passport number |
| 出発地 | coming from |
| 目的地 | going to |
| 日付 | date |
| 署名 | signature |

accommodation

# * hotels, inns and hostels

● Budget Japanese-style accommodation is available at family-run guest houses 民宿 (min shuku). Meals are communal and the facilities are shared. Some Buddhist temples 宿坊 (shukuboh), receive paying guests, where you can also meditate with the monks and eat *shohjin ryohri*. Japan has a network of youth hostels, see the website of the Japan Youth Hostel Association www.jyh.or.jp/english/index.html

## YOU MAY WANT TO SAY...

| | | |
|---|---|---|
| ● Where can I park? | 駐車場はどこですか？ | chuusha joh wa doko des ka |
| ● May I see the room please? | 部屋を見せていただけますか？ | heya o misete itadake mas ka |
| ● Do you have... | …はありますか？ | ...wa arimas ka |
| a room with a view? | 眺めの良い部屋 | nagame no ii heya |
| a bigger room? | もっと広い部屋 | motto hiroi heya |
| a cot for the baby? | ベビーベッド | bebii beddo |
| ● I've booked a room... | …の部屋を予約しました | ...no heya o yoyaku shima shita |
| with a garden | 庭付き | niwa tsuki |
| with a private outdoor bath | 露天風呂付き | roten buro tsuki |
| ● What time... | …は何時ですか？ | ...wa nanji des ka |
| is breakfast? | 朝食 | choh shoku |
| do you lock the front door? | 玄関が閉まるの | genkan ga shimaru no |

| English | 日本語 | Rōmaji |
|---|---|---|
| Where is/are... | …はどこですか? | ...wa doko des ka |
| the dining room? | 食堂/レストラン | shokudoh/resutoran |
| the bar? | バー | bah |
| the bathroom? | お風呂 | o furo |
| the toilets? | トイレ | toire |
| Is there... | …はありますか? | ...wa arimas ka? |
| 24-hour room service? | 二十四時間のルームサービス | nijuu yojikan no ruumu sahbisu |
| an internet connection in my room ? | 部屋にインターネットの接続 | heya ni intah netto no setsuzoku |
| a business centre here? | デスクワークのできる部屋 | desuku wahku no dekiru heya |
| a fitness centre here? | ヘルスクラブ | herusu kurabu |
| Are there any more ... | …がありますか | ...ga arimas ka? |
| blankets? | もっと毛布 | motto mohfu |
| When will you ... | …はいつですか | ...wa itsu des ka? |
| lay out the bedding? | 布団をしくの | futon o shiku no |
| start serving dinner? | 夕食が出るの | yuushoku ga deru no |
| clear away the bedding? | 布団を片付けるの | futon o katazukeru no |
| May I borrow a... | …を貸して下さい | ...o kashite kudasai |
| hair dryer? | ドライヤー | doraiyah |
| umbrella? | 傘 | kasa |
| How can I contact you? | どうやって連絡がとれますか。 | dohyatte renraku ga tore mas ka? |

accommodation

### YOU MAY HEAR...

| | | |
|---|---|---|
| 駐車場は… あります | *chuusha joh wa... arimas* | The car park is... |
| 駐車場入口のコード番号です。 | *chuusha joh iriguchi no kohdo bangoh des* | Here's the code for the car park. |
| 申し訳ございませんが、本日空いている部屋がございません。 | *mohshi wake gozai masen ga, honjitsu aiteiru heya ga gozai masen* | I'm afraid we have no rooms left for tonight. |
| 明日、お部屋をお取替えできるかもしれません。 | *asu, oheya o otori kae dekiru kamo shire masen* | We might be able to change your room tomorrow. |
| 朝食は… から…までです | *choh shoku wa... kara... ma de des* | Breakfast is from... to... |
| 夕食は … 準備致します<br> この部屋に<br> 七時から | *yuu shoku wa ... junbi itashi mas*<br> *kono heya ni*<br> *shichiji kara* | Dinner will be served...<br> in this room<br> from 7pm |
| 正面玄関は… に閉まります。 | *shohmen genkan wa... ni shimari mas* | We lock the front door at... |
| こちらへどうぞ。 | *kochira e dohzo* | Follow me, please. |
| はい。二十四時間のルームサービスがございます。 | *hai. nijuu yojikan no ruumu sahbisu ga gozai mas* | Yes, there's 24-hour room service. |
| インターネットの接続はお部屋でできます。 | *intah netto no setsuzoku wa oheya de deki mas* | There's an internet connection in your room. |

| | | |
|---|---|---|
| お茶とお菓子をご用意致しました。 | *ocha to okashi o goyohi itashi mashita* | Here are complimentary Japanese tea and biscuits. |
| 押入れに予備の毛布/枕がございます。 | *oshi ire ni yobi no mohfu/makura ga gozai mas* | There are spare blankets/pillows in the cupboard. |
| この電話で「ゼロ」を押して下さい。 | *kono denwa de 'zero' o oshite kudasai* | Please use this telephone and dial '0'. |
| 布団は夕食の後、準備致します。 | *futon wa yuu shoku no ato junbi itashi mas* | Your bedding will be laid out after dinner. |
| 大浴場はいつでもお入りになれます。 | *dai yokujoh wa itsu demo ohairi ni nare mas* | The communal bathroom is open 24 hours-a-day. |

# ✳ camping
(see **directions**, page 52)

● Campsites are strategically located throughout Japan, in proximity to places of interest. There are two types of campsites: *ohto* (オート) and *tento* (テント). At an 'auto' camp, you can leave your car by your tent; at a 'tent' camp, you leave it in the car park.

accommodation

## YOU MAY WANT TO SAY...

- Is there ... round here?
  - a campsite
  - a place to fish

  - a hot spring

この辺に … はありますか？
　キャンプ場
　つりのできる場所

温泉

*konohen ni... wa arimas ka*
　*kyanpu joh*
　*tsuri no dekiru basho*
　*onsen*

- Can we camp here?

ここでキャンプはできますか？

*koko de kyanpu wa deki mas ka*

- What's the charge?

いくらですか？

*ikura des ka*

- It's a two/four-person tent.

二人/四人用のテントです。

*futari/yonin yoh no tento des*

- Where is/are...
  - the toilets?
  - the showers?
  - the dustbins?
  - the laundrette?
  - the public telephone?

…はどこですか？
　トイレ
　シャワー
　ごみ箱
　コインランドリー
　公衆電話

*...wa doko des ka*
　*toire*
　*shawah*
　*gomi bako*
　*koin randorii*
　*kohshuu denwa*

- Is this water drinkable?

これは飲料水ですか？

*korewa inryoh sui des ka*

- Where is/are the power point/s?

コンセントはどこですか？

*konsento wa doko des ka*

- Is there a children's playground?

子供の遊び場がありますか？

*kodomo no asobiba ga arimas ka*

accommodation

## YOU MAY HEAR...

| | | |
|---|---|---|
| 一番近くのキャンプ場は… | ichiban chikaku no kyanpu joh wa... | The nearest campsite is... |
| 五キロ離れています | gokiro hanarete imas | five kilometres away |
| 隣の村にあります | tonari no mura ni arimas | in the next village |
| 地図を持っていますか? | chizu o motte imas ka | Have you got a map? |
| ここでキャンプはできません。 | koko de kyanpu wa deki masen | You can't camp here. |
| 管理棟は… 開いています | kanri toh wa... aite imas | The site office is open... |
| 午前八時から午後５時まで | gozen hachiji kara gogo goji ma de | from 8am to 5pm |
| ごみは持ち帰って下さい。 | gomi wa mochi kaette kudasai | Please remove all your rubbish. |
| シャワーは五分三百円です。 | shawah wa gofun sanbyaku en des | It's ¥300 for each 5 minutes in the shower. |
| 洗濯機は一回二百円です。 | sentakuki wa ikkai nihyaku en des | It's ¥200 to use the washing machine. |
| 小さい公園があります。 | chiisai kohen ga arimas | There's a small playground. |
| コンセントはあちらにあります。 | konsento wa achira ni arimas | The power point is over there. |

## \* requests and queries

### YOU MAY WANT TO SAY...

| | | |
|---|---|---|
| Are there any messages for me? | 私に伝言がありますか？ | watashi ni dengon ga arimas ka |
| Is there a fax for me? | 私にファックスが届いていますか？ | watashi ni fakkusu ga todoite imas ka |
| I'm expecting... <br> a phone call <br> a fax | …を待っています <br> 電話 <br> ファックス | ... o matte imas <br> denwa <br> fakkusu |
| Can I... <br> leave this in the safe? <br> put it on my room bill? | …もらえますか？ <br> 貴重品をあずかって <br> 部屋代と一緒につけておいて | ...morae mas ka <br> kichoh hin o azukatte <br> heya dai to isshoni tsukete oite |
| Can you... <br> bring my things from the safe? <br> wake me up at eight o'clock? <br> call a taxi for me? <br> come back later, please? | …もらえますか？ <br> 預けた貴重品を出して <br> 八時にモーニングコールをして <br> タクシーを呼んで <br> 後でまた来て | ...morae mas ka <br> azuketa kichohhin o dashite <br> hachiji ni mohningu kohru o shite <br> takushii o yonde <br> atode mata kite |
| Do you have a babysitting service? | ベビーシッターのサービスがありますか？ | bebii shittah no sahbisu ga arimas ka |
| I need... <br> another pillow <br> an adaptor | …がいるんですが… <br> もう一つ枕 <br> アダプター | ...ga irun des ga... <br> moh hitotsu makura <br> adaputah |
| Is there a disabled toilet? | 障害者用のトイレがありますか？ | shohgaisha yoh no toire ga arimas ka? |

| | | |
|---|---|---|
| I've lost my key. | 鍵をなくしてしまいました。 | *kagi o nakushite shimai mashita* |
| I've left my key in the room. | 部屋に鍵を忘れてしまいました。 | *heya ni kagi o wasurete shimai mashita* |
| I/We want to stay another night. | もう一泊したいんですが。 | *moh ippaku shitain des ga* |
| I/We want to check-out one day early. | 一日早くチェックアウトしたいんですが。 | *ichi nichi hayaku chekku auto shitain des ga* |

## YOU MAY HEAR...

| | | |
|---|---|---|
| お客様に伝言/ファックスがございます。 | *okyaku sama ni dengon/fakkusu ga gozaimas* | There's a message/fax for you. |
| いいえ。お客様に伝言はございません。 | *iie. okyaku sama ni dengon wa gozai masen* | No, there are no messages for you. |
| モーニングコールを致しましょうか? | *mohningu kohru o itashi masho ka* | Would you like a wake-up call? |
| 何時がよろしいですか? | *nanji ga yoroshii des ka* | (For) what time? |
| いつベビーシッターが必要ですか? | *itsu bebii shittah ga hitsu yoh des ka* | When would you like the babysitter to come? |
| 少々お待ち下さい。 | *shoh shoh omachi kudasai* | Just a moment, please. |

accommodation

## ✳ problems and complaints

### YOU MAY WANT TO SAY...

| | | |
|---|---|---|
| Excuse me. | すみません。 | sumimasen |
| The room is... | 部屋が | heya ga |
| too hot | 暑すぎます | atsusugi mas |
| too cold | 寒すぎます | samu sugi mas |
| too small | 狭すぎます | sema sugi mas |
| too noisy | うるさすぎます | urusa sugi mas |
| There isn't any... | …がありません | ...ga arimasen |
| toilet paper | トイレットペーパー | toiretto peipah |
| hot water | お湯 | oyu |
| soap | 石鹸 | sekken |
| There aren't any... | …がありません | ...ga arimasen |
| slippers | スリッパ | surippa |
| towels | タオル | taoru |
| I can't... | …ないんですが。 | ...nain des ga |
| open the window | 窓があか | mado ga aka |
| turn off the tap | 蛇口が締まら | jaguchi ga shimara |
| turn on the TV | テレビがつか | terebi ga tsuka |
| The bed is uncomfortable. | ベッドの具合がよくありません。 | beddo no guai ga yoku arimasen |
| The bathroom is dirty. | 浴室が汚れています. | yoku shitsu ga yogorete imas |
| The toilet won't flush. | トイレが流れません。 | toire ga nagare masen |
| ...is not working. | …が使えません。 | ...ga tsukae masen |
| The shower | シャワー | shawah |
| The air-conditioning | エアコン | eakon |

- **I can smell gas.** ガスのにおいがします。 *gasu no nioi ga shimas*

- **Please send someone up.** 誰かをよこして下さい。 *dareka o yokoshite kudasai*

- **I want to see the manager!** 責任者を呼んで下さい。 *sekinin sha o yonde kudasai*

### YOU MAY HEAR...

| | | |
|---|---|---|
| 少々お待ち下さい。 | *shoh shoh omachi kudasai* | Just a moment, please. |
| もちろんです。 | *mochiron des* | Of course. |
| すぐに別の物をお持ちします。 | *sugu ni betsu no mono o omochi shimas* | I'll bring you another one, immediately. |
| 担当の者がすぐにお部屋に伺います。 | *tantoh no mono ga sugu ni oheya ni ukagai mas* | I'll send someone in charge immediately. |
| 明日修理いたします。 | *asu shuuri itashi mas* | I'll fix it for you tomorrow. |
| 申し訳ありませんが、今日中は、難しいです。 | *mohshi wake arimasen ga, kyoh juu wa muzukashii des* | I'm sorry, it's not possible today. |
| 申し訳ございませんが、お手伝いできることが、ありません。 | *mohshi wake gozai masen ga, otetsudai dekirukoto ga arimasen* | I'm sorry, there's nothing we can do. |

accommodation

# ✳ checking out

## YOU MAY WANT TO SAY...

- The bill, please.

  清算をお願いします。

  *seisan o onegai shimas*

- I'd like to...
  pay the bill and check-out
  stay another night

  …したいんですが
  支払いとチェックアウトを
  もう一泊

  *...shitain des ga*
  *shiharai to chekku auto o*
  *moh ippaku*

- What time is check-out?

  チェックアウトは何時ですか?

  *chekku auto wa nanji des ka*

- May I...
  have a late check-out?

  leave my luggage here?

  …できますか?
  チェックアウトを遅くすることが

  ここに荷物を預けることが

  *...deki mas ka*
  *chekku auto o osoku suru koto ga*

  *koko ni nimotsu o azukeru koto ga*

- There's a mistake in the bill.

  請求書に間違いがあるんですが…。

  *seikyuusho ni machigai ga arun des ga...*

- I/We've had a great time.

  とても楽しかったです。

  *totemo tanoshi katta des*

## YOU MAY HEAR...

- チェックアウトは十一時です。

  *chekku auto wa juuichi ji des*

  Check-out is at eleven o'clock.

- …までお部屋をお使いいただけます。

  *...made oheya o otsukai itadake mas*

  You can have the room until...

| | | |
|---|---|---|
| お荷物はいくつありますか?。 | onimotsu wa ikutsu arimas ka | How many bags? |
| こちらでお預かりします。 | kochira de oazukari shimas | Leave them here. |
| ポーターがお運びします。 | pohtah ga ohakobi shimas | The porter will put them away. |
| 確認いたします。 | kakunin itashi mas | Let me check it. |
| どうぞ、またお越し下さい。 | dohzo mata okoshi kudasai | Come again! |

## ✳ self-catering

(see **problems and complaints**, page 92)

**YOU MAY WANT TO SAY...**

| | | |
|---|---|---|
| I've rented... an apartment | …を借りました アパート | ...o kari mashita apahto |
| Can you give me the key, please? | 鍵をお願いします。 | kagi o onegai shimas |
| Where is... the fuse box? | …はどこですか? ブレーカー | ...wa doko des ka bureh kah |
| How does the ... work? cooker hot water | …はどうやって使うんですか? ガスレンジ 湯沸かし器 | ...wa doh yatte tsukau n des ka gasu renji yuwakashi ki |
| Is/Are there... air-conditioning? any shops round here? | …はありますか? エアコン この辺に店 | ...wa arimas ka eakon konohen ni mise |

accommodation

95

| | | |
|---|---|---|
| ● **Where do I/we put the rubbish?** | どこにごみを出したらいいですか？ | *doko ni gomi o dashitara iides ka* |
| ● **May I borrow...** | …をお借りできますか？ | *...o okari deki mas ka* |
| **a corkscrew?** | ワインの栓抜き | *wain no sen nuki* |
| ● **How can I contact you?** | どうやって連絡が取れますか？ | *doh yatte renraku ga toremas ka* |

## YOU MAY HEAR... ②

| | | |
|---|---|---|
| 使用説明書は、ガスレンジ/ボイラーのそばにあります。 | *setsumei sho wa, gasu renji/boirah no soba ni arimas* | **The instructions are by the cooker/ boiler.** |
| このようにすると作動します。 | *kono yohni suruto sadoh shimas* | **It works like this.** |
| このボタン/スイッチを押してください。 | *kono botan/suicchi o oshite kudasai* | **Press this button/ switch.** |
| 押入れに予備の毛布/枕があります。 | *oshiire ni yobi no mohfu/makura ga arimas* | **There are spare blankets/pillows in the cupboard.** |
| ごみはごみ箱にすててください。 | *gomi wa gomi bako ni sutete kudasai* | **Put the rubbish in the dustbin.** |
| ごみの日は金曜日です。 | *gomi no hi wa kin yohbi des* | **The rubbish is collected on Fridays.** |
| 掃除の者は … に伺います。 | *sohji no mono wa... ni ukagai mas* | **The cleaner comes on...** |
| 私の携帯番号は … です。 | *watashi no keitai bangoh wa ... des* | **My mobile number is...** |

# food&drink

# * food and drink

Meals are eaten early in Japan: breakfast from 07:00, lunch from 12:00, and dinner from 18:30. Restaurants are very child-friendly; ファミリーレストラン ('family restaurants') specialise in serving a wide range of Japanese, Chinese and Western dishes.

## YOU MAY SEE...

| | | |
|---|---|---|
| バー | *bah* | bar |
| カラオケバー | *karaoke bah* | karaoke bar |
| ハンバーガーショップ | *hanbahgah shoppu* | burger bar |
| カフェ/喫茶店 | *kafe/kissa ten* | café |
| インターネットカフェ | *intah netto kafe* | internet café |
| コーヒーショップ/珈琲店 | *Koh hii shoppu/koh hii ten* | coffee house |
| 飲み屋/居酒屋 | *nomiya/izakaya* | pub |
| レストラン/料理店 | *resutoran/ryohri ten* | restaurant |
| 日本料理 | *nihon ryohri* | Japanese |
| 中華/中国料理 | *chuuka/chuugoku ryohri* | Chinese |
| フランス料理 | *furansu ryohri* | French |
| イタリア料理 | *itaria ryohri* | Italian |
| 韓国料理 | *kan koku ryohri* | Korean |
| タイ料理 | *tai ryohri* | Thai |
| ティールーム/喫茶店 | *tii ruumu/kissa ten* | tea room |
| 飲み放題 | *nomi hohdai* | all you can drink |
| 食べ放題 | *tabe hohdai* | all you can eat |

| | | |
|---|---|---|
| バイキング | *baikingu* | **buffet/self-service** |
| 日替りランチ | *hi gawari ranchi* | **daily set-lunch** |
| 日替りディナー | *hi gawari dinah* | **daily set-dinner** |
| 郷土料理 | *kyohdo ryohri* | **regional cuisine** |
| ディナーセット | *dinah setto* | **set-dinner** |
| ランチセット | *ranchi setto* | **set-lunch** |
| セットメニュー | *setto menyuu* | **set menu** |
| 持ち帰り | *mochi kaeri* | **take-away** |
| 回転ずし | *kaiten zushi* | **sushi (conveyor belt)** |
| ラーメン屋 | *rahmen ya* | **ramen** |
| お好み焼屋 | *okonomi yaki ya* | **okonomiyaki restaurant** |
| そば屋 | *soba ya* | **Japanese soba noodle restaurant** |
| うどん屋 | *udon ya* | **Japanese udon noodle restaurant** |
| 焼肉屋 | *yakiniku ya* | **Korean style barbeque** |
| 焼き鳥屋 | *yakitori ya* | **Japanese grilled chicken restaurant** |

# ✳ making bookings
(see **time phrases**, page 21)

● Bookings can be made for larger groups and at popular restaurants in the evenings; in general, however, bookings are less common for most things in Japan, including restaurants.

food and drink

## YOU MAY WANT TO SAY...

- I'd like to reserve a table for...
  …席を予約したいんですが…
  *...seki o yoyaku shita in des ga...*

  two people
  二人分の
  *futari bun no*

  two adults and three children
  大人二人と子供三人分の
  *otona futari to kodomo san nin bun no*

  tomorrow evening at half-past eight
  明日の晩、八時半に
  *asu no ban, hachiji han ni*

  this evening at nine o'clock
  今晩九時に、
  *konban, kuji ni*

- My name is...
  （私の名前は）…です。
  *(watashi no namae wa) ... des*

- My telephone/ mobile number is...
  私の電話/携帯の番号は … です
  *watashi no denwa/ keitai no bangoh wa ... des*

- Could you book us a table...
  …席の予約をしていただけますか?
  *...seki no yoyaku o shite itadake mas ka*

  earlier?
  もう少し早い時間に
  *moh sukoshi hayai jikan ni*

  later?
  もう少し遅い時間に
  *moh sukoshi osoi jikan ni*

## YOU MAY HEAR...

- 何時にお席をご用意しましょうか?
  *nan ji ni oseki o goyohi shimashoh ka*
  What time would you like the table for?

- 何名様ですか?
  *nan mei sama des ka*
  For how many people?

| お名前をお願いします？ | onamae o onegai shimas | **What's your name?** |
| お電話番号をお願いいします？ | o denwa bangoh o onegai shimas | **What's your telephone number?** |
| 申し訳ございませんが、満席です。 | mohshiwake gozai masenga, manseki des | **I'm sorry we're fully booked.** |

## ✳ at the restaurant
(see **bars and cafés**, page 107)

● Japanese restaurants are often small family affairs, many are called 屋 (ya) which literally means shop. They often specialise in a particular dish, e.g., sushi, tempura, or type of cooking, with distinct regional variations and an emphasis on seasonal ingredients. Western cuisine, 洋食, (yohshoku), is widely available, though sauces and recipes often have a Japanese twist.

### YOU MAY WANT TO SAY...

| **I've booked a table.** | 席を予約してあります。 | seki o yoyaku shite arimas |
| **My name is...** | 私の名前は…です。 | watashi no namae wa... des |
| **We haven't booked.** | 予約してないんですが…。 | yoyaku shite nain des ga... |
| **A table for four, please.** | 四人です。 | yonin des |

**food and drink**

101

| | | |
|---|---|---|
| **A ... room, if possible** | 出来たら … をお願いします | *deki tara ... o onegai shimas* |
| Japanese-style | 和室 | *washitsu* |
| private dining | 個室 | *koshitsu* |
| **Do you have a high chair?** | 子供用の椅子はありますか? | *kodomo yoh no isu wa arimas ka* |
| **How long is the wait?** | 待ち時間はどのくらいですか? | *machi jikan wa dono kurai des ka* |
| **Do you take credit cards?** | クレジットカードが使えますか? | *kurejitto kahdo ga tsukae mas ka* |

## YOU MAY HEAR...

| | | |
|---|---|---|
| ご予約はございますか? | *goyoyaku wa gozai mas ka* | Have you got a reservation? |
| どちらの席がよろしいですか? | *dochira no seki ga yoroshii des ka* | Where would you like to sit? |
| たばこをお吸いになりますか? | *tabako o osuini narimas ka* | Smoking or non-smoking? |
| 少々お待ち下さい。 | *shoh shoh omachi kudasai* | Just a moment, please. |
| お待ちになりますか? | *omachi ni narimas ka* | Would you care to wait? |
| 申し訳ございませんが、… | *mohshiwake gozaimasenga ...* | I'm sorry we're ... |
| 満席です | *manseki des* | full |
| 閉店しました | *heiten shima shita* | closed |
| クレジットカードは使えません。 | *kurejitto kahdo wa tsukae masen* | We don't accept credit cards. |

food and drink

102

# ✳ ordering your food

● Many restaurants display plastic samples outside their entrances to show what's on offer. Menus often include photos of dishes as well.

● Food is available à la carte or as set meals 定食 (*tei shoku*). The dishes are served at the same time, as there are no distinct courses.

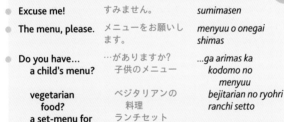

## YOU MAY WANT TO SAY...

| | | |
|---|---|---|
| Excuse me! | すみません。 | *sumimasen* |
| The menu, please. | メニューをお願いします。 | *menyuu o onegai shimas* |
| Do you have... a child's menu? | …がありますか? 子供のメニュー | *...ga arimas ka kodomo no menyuu* |
| vegetarian food? | ベジタリアンの料理 | *bejitarian no ryohri* |
| a set-menu for lunch? | ランチセット | *ranchi setto* |
| Is it self-service? | セルフサービスですか? | *serufu sahbisu des ka* |
| We're ready to order. | 注文をお願いします。 | *chuumon o onegai shimas* |
| I'd like... | …をお願いします | *...o onegai shimas* |
| May I have...? more water green tea | …をいただけますか? もっと水 お茶 | *...o itadake mas ka motto mizu ocha* |

**food and drink**

| | | |
|---|---|---|
| **What's this, please?** | これは何ですか? | *kore wa nan des ka* |
| **What are today's specials?** | 今日のおすすめは何 ですか? | *kyoh no osusume wa nan des ka* |
| **What's the local speciality?** | 地元の名物は何で すか? | *jimoto no meibutsu wa nan des ka* |
| **I'll have the same as him/her/them.** | 彼/彼女/彼らと同じ 物をお願いします。 | *kare/kanojo/karera to onaji mono o onegai shimas* |
| **I'd like it...**<br>rare<br>medium<br>well done | …でお願いします。<br>レア<br>ミディアム<br>ウェルダン | *...de onegai shimas*<br>*rea*<br>*midiamu*<br>*uerudan* |
| **Excuse me, I've changed my mind.** | すみません、注文を かえられますか。 | *sumimasen, chuumon o kaerare mas ka?* |

## YOU MAY HEAR...

| | | |
|---|---|---|
| まず、お飲み物は いかがですか? | *mazu, onomi mono wa ikaga des ka* | **Would you like a drink first?** |
| ご注文はお決まり ですか。 | *gochuumon wa okimari des ka* | **Are you ready to order?** |
| …をおすすめしま す | *...o osusume shimas* | **We recommend...** |
| 他にご注文はござ いますか? | *hoka ni gochuumon wa gozai mas ka* | **Anything else?** |
| 焼き加減はどのよ うになさいますか? | *yaki kagen wa dono yohni nasai mas ka* | **How would you like it cooked?** |

| | | |
|---|---|---|
| …はいかがですか? | …wa ikaga des ka | Would you like some… |
| コーヒー | koh hii | coffee? |
| お茶 | ocha | green tea? |
| デザートのメニューをご覧になりますか? | dezahto no menyuu o goran ni narimas ka | Would you like to see the dessert menu? |
| ご注文は以上でよろしいでしょうか。 | gochuumon wa ijoh de yoroshii deshoh ka? | Is that all you would like to order? |

## ✳ ordering your drinks

● Most restaurants and bars offer a range of Japanese and imported alcoholic drinks. The majority of wine is imported. The national rice wine, sake (酒) is also known as nihon shu (日本酒). There are nearly 2,000 sake brewers and 10,000 different types of sake brewed in Japan. Sake is served warm in the winter and chilled in summer.

● Ordering mineral water is uncommon. Tap water and tea お茶 (ocha) are offered (without charge) once you are seated.

● When drinking (in public) in a group, the custom in Japan is to pour for others and then allow them to pour for you. The toast is kanpai (乾杯).

food and drink

## YOU MAY WANT TO SAY...

| | | |
|---|---|---|
| Can we see the wine list, please? | ワインリストを見せてもらえますか? | *wain risuto o misete morae mas ka* |
| What wines do you have? | どんなワインがありますか? | *don na wain ga arimas ka* |
| We'll have the house red/white, please. | ハウスワインの赤/白をお願いします。 | *hausu wain no aka/ shiro o onegai shimas* |
| A bottle of this please. | これをボトルでお願いします。 | *koreo botoru de onegai shimas* |
| Do you have a list of the sakes you serve? | 日本酒のリストはありますか? | *nihonshu no risuto wa arimas ka* |
| Is there a local sake? | 地元のお酒はありますか?。 | *jimoto no osake wa arimas ka* |
| Can I have some hot sake, please? | お酒を熱燗でもらえますか。 | *osake o atsukan de morae mas ka* |
| What beers do you have? | どんなビールがありますか? | *don na biiru ga arimas ka* |
| Can I have draught beer? | 生ビールをお願いします | *nama biiru o onegai shimas* |
| I'll have... a gin and tonic a vodka and coke whisky | …をお願いします。 ジントニック ウオッカをコーラで割ったもの ウイスキー | *...o onegai shimas jin tonikku uokka o kohra de watta mono ui sukii* |
| What soft drinks do you have? | どんなソフトドリンクがありますか? | *don na sofuto dorinku ga arimas ka* |

food and drink

106

## YOU MAY HEAR...

| | | |
|---|---|---|
| かしこまりました。 | *kashiko mari mashita* | **Certainly.** |
| こちらです。 | *kochira des* | **Here it is.** |
| 氷とレモンをお入れしますか? | *kohri to remon o oire shimas ka* | **Would you like ice and lemon?** |
| 水割りになさいますか? | *mizu wari ni nasai mas ka* | **Would you like some water?** |
| コーラ、ジュース、レモネード、アイスティー、アイスコーヒーがございます。 | *kohra, juusu, remo neido, aisu tii, aisu koh hii ga gozai mas* | **We have coke, juices, lemonade, iced tea and iced coffee.** |

## ✳ bars and cafés

● Traditional Japanese-style pubs *izakaya* (居酒屋) and *akachohchin* (赤ちょうちん) are identifiable by their red paper lanterns, which act like British pub signs.

## YOU MAY WANT TO SAY...

| | | |
|---|---|---|
| I'll have... please | …をお願いします | *...o onegai shimas* |
| a coffee | コーヒー | *koh hii* |
| a white coffee | ミルクコーヒー | *miruku koh hii* |
| a black coffee | ブラックコーヒー | *burakku de koh hii* |
| a cup of tea | 紅茶 | *koh cha* |
| a fruit/herbal tea | フルーツ/ハーブティー | *furuutsu/hah bu tii* |

| | | |
|---|---|---|
| ● with milk/lemon | ミルク/レモンで | *miruku/remon de* |
| ● A glass of... | …を一杯 | *...o ippai* |
|    tap water | 水 | *mizu* |
|    beer | ビール | *biiru* |
|    cold sake | 冷酒 | *reishu* |
|    wine | ワイン | *wain* |
|    apple juice | アップルジュース | *appuru juusu* |
| ● A piece of chocolate cake, please. | チョコレートケーキを一つお願いします。 | *chokoreito keiki o hitotsu onegai shimas* |
| ● What kind of ...do you have? | どんな… がありますか? | *don na ... ga arimas ka* |
|    sandwiches | サンドイッチ | *sando icchi* |
|    cakes | ケーキ | *keiki* |
|    salads | サラダ | *sarada* |
|    pizzas | ピザ | *piza* |
| ● Is there any... | …はありますか? | *...wa arimas ka* |
|    pepper? | こしょう | *koshoh* |
|    salt? | 塩 | *shio* |
|    soy sauce? | 醤油 | *shohyu* |
|    tomato ketchup? | ケチャップ | *kechappu* |
| ● Same again, please. | 同じものをもう一つお願いします。 | *onaji mono o moh hitotsu onegai shimas* |
| ● How much is that? | それはいくらですか? | *sore wa ikura des ka* |

## YOU MAY HEAR...

| | | |
|---|---|---|
| ご注文は何になさいますか? | gochuumon wa nani ni nasai mas ka | What would you like? |
| 大きいのと小さいのとどちらがよろしいですか? | ohkii no to chiisai noto dochiraga yoroshii des ka | What size would you like: large or small? |
| 氷はお入れしますか? | kohri wa oire shimas ka | Would you like ice? |
| お支払いはご一緒ですか、別々ですか? | oshiharai wa goissho des ka, betsubetsu des ka | Are you paying together or separately? |

## ✻ comments and requests

### YOU MAY WANT TO SAY...

| | | |
|---|---|---|
| This is delicious! | おいしいです。 | oishii des |
| Can we have more... | …をもっといただけますか? | ...o motto ita dake mas ka |
| water, please? | 水 | mizu |
| green tea, please? | お茶 | ocha |
| Can we have... please? | … をお願いします。 | ...o onegai shimas |
| another bottle of wine | もう一本ワイン | moh ippon wain |
| another glass | もう一杯お代り | moh ippai okawari |
| another bowl of rice | もう一杯ご飯 | moh ippai gohan |
| I couldn't eat another thing. | もうお腹が一杯です。 | moh onakaga ippai des |

food and drink

| | | |
|---|---|---|
| ご注文は以上でしょうか？ | gochuumon wa ijoh de shoh ka | Will that be all? |
| ご注文はお揃いですか？ | gochuumon wa osoroi des ka | Is everything all right? |
| お食事はいかがでしたか。 | oshokuji wa ikaga deshita ka? | Did you enjoy your meal? |

## ✳ special requirements

● If you're a strict vegetarian, check the sauces and soup stocks, which often contain *katsuo bushi* or *ni boshi* (dried tuna flakes, dried sardines).

● There is a well-established tradition of Buddhist vegetarian cooking 精進料理 *(shohjin ryhori)* best experienced at the temples in and around Kyoto. Authentic *shohjin ryhori* is served without alcohol, garlic, onions or leeks, and includes five dishes *(okazu)*.

YOU MAY WANT TO SAY...

| | | |
|---|---|---|
| I'm diabetic. | 糖尿病なんです。 | toh nyoh byoh nan des |
| I'm allergic to... | …のアレルギーがあります | ...no arerugii ga arimas |
| cow's milk | 牛乳 | gyuu nyuu |
| eggs | 卵 | tamago |
| nuts | ナッツ | nattsu |
| shellfish | 貝類 | kai rui |

| | | |
|---|---|---|
| • I'm vegetarian. | ベジタリアンです。 | *bejitarian des* |
| • I don't eat meat or fish. | 肉や魚を食べません。 | *niku ya sakana o tabe masen* |
| • I don't eat any animal products. | 動物性食品は全く食べません。 | *dohbutsu sei shokuhin wa mattaku tabemasen* |
| • I can't eat... | …が食べられません。 | *...ga taberare masen* |
|     dairy products | 乳製品 | *nyuu seihin* |
|     wheat products | 小麦製品 | *komugi seihin* |
| • Do you have ... food? | …食べ物はありますか? | *...tabemono wa arimas ka* |
|     low sodium | 塩分の少ない | *enbun no sukunai* |
|     low-fat | 低脂肪の | *tei shiboh no* |
| • Do you have anything without meat? | 肉が入っていないメニューがありますか? | *niku ga haitte inai menyuu ga arimas ka* |
| • Does it contain... | …が入っていますか? | *... ga haitte imas ka* |
|     butter? | バター | *batah* |
|     dried tuna flakes? | 鰹節 | *katsuo bushi* |
|     garlic? | にんにく | *nin niku* |
|     sesame oil? | 胡麻油 | *goma abura* |
| • Does that have dried sardines in it? | その中に煮干が入っていますか? | *sono naka ni niboshi ga haitte imas ka* |

food and drink

111

| | | |
|---|---|---|
| 調理場に確認して みます。 | *chohriba ni kakunin shite mimas* | **I'll check with the kitchen.** |
| そちらには ... が入っています | *sochira niwa ... ga haitte imas* | **It's got ... in it** |

# ✳ problems and complaints

YOU MAY WANT TO SAY...

| | | |
|---|---|---|
| **Excuse me.** | すみません。 | *sumimasen* |
| **This is...** | これは... | *kore wa...* |
| burnt | 焦げています | *kogete imas* |
| cold | 冷めています | *samete imas* |
| dry | パサパサしています | *pasa pasa shite imas* |
| under-cooked | 生焼けです | *nama yake des* |
| **I didn't order this.** | これは注文していません。 | *kore wa chuumon shite imasen* |
| **I ordered ...** | …を注文しました。 | *...o chuumon shima shita* |
| **Is our food coming soon?** | 私たちの料理はもうすぐ来ますか? | *watashi tachi no ryohri wa mohsugu kimas ka* |

# ✱ paying the bill

● You will need to request the bill at the end of your meal, it's rude in Japan to give it to you unsolicited. In many restaurants you pay a cashier on departing. If you are eating in a formal group, the host usually pays. Tipping is not expected.

## YOU MAY WANT TO SAY...

● **The bill, please.**
お勘定をお願いします。
*okanjyoh o onegai shimas*

● **There's a mistake here.**
これは間違いだと思うんですが…。
*kore wa machigai dato omou n des ga…*

● **That was fantastic, thank you.**
とてもおいしかったです。ごちそうさまでした。
*totemo oishi katta des. gochisoh sama deshita*

## YOU MAY HEAR...

● サービス料は含まれています。
*sahbisu ryoh wa fuku marete imas*
**Service is included.**

● 申し訳ありませんが、現金のみのお支払いとなります。
*mohshi wake arimasen ga, genkin nomi no oshiharai to nari mas*
**Sorry, we only accept cash.**

● ありがとうございました。
*arigatoh gozai mashita*
**Thank you.**

**food and drink**

# ✳ buying food

● Vending machines offer a variety of food and drinks, as well as non-consumables.

● Japan's ultimate convenience food is the *bentoh* (弁当), a lunch box, available everywhere to suit all price ranges.

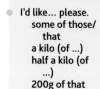

| | | |
|---|---|---|
| **I'd like... please.** | …お願いします。 | *..onegai shimas* |
| some of those/that | それを | *sore o* |
| a kilo (of ...) | …を1キロ | *...o ichi kiro* |
| half a kilo (of ...) | …を500グラム | *...o go hyaku guramu* |
| 200g of that | それを200グラム | *sore o nihyaku guramu* |
| a piece of that | それを一つ | *sore o hitotsu* |
| two slices of that | それを二枚 | *sore o nimai* |
| **How much is... that?** | …はいくらですか? それ | *...wa ikura des ka sore* |
| **What's that, please?** | それは何ですか? | *sore wa nan des ka* |
| **Have you got...** | …はありますか? | *...wa arimas ka* |
| lunch boxes? | 弁当 | *bentoh* |
| sushi? | すし | *sushi* |
| soba noodles? | そば | *soba* |
| rice balls? | おにぎり | *onigiri* |
| **A bit more, please.** | もう少しお願いします。 | *moh sukoshi onegai shimas* |

- A bit less, please. | もう 少し少なくして 下さい。 | *moh sukoshi sukunaku shite kudasai*

- That's enough, thank you. | それで充分です。ありがとう。 | *sorede juubun des. arigatoh*

- That's all, thank you. | それで全部です。ありがとう。 | *sore de zenbu des. arigatoh*

- I'm looking for the ... section | …のコーナーを探しているんですが | *...no koh nah o sagashite iru n des ga*
  dairy | 乳製品 | *nyuu seihin*
  fruit and vegetable | 野菜と果物 | *yasai to kuda momo*

- Can I have a bag, please? | 袋をいただけますか。 | *fukuro o itadake mas ka*

## YOU MAY HEAR...

| いらっしゃいませ。 | *irasshai mase* | Can I help you? |
| 何になさいますか？ | *nani ni nasai mas ka* | What would you like? |
| どのくらい致しましょうか？ | *donokurai itashimashoh ka* | How much would you like? |
| おいくつ致しましょうか？ | *o ikutsu itashimashoh ka* | How many would you like? |
| 申し訳ありません 売り切れました。 | *moh shiwake ari masen, uri kire mashita* | I'm sorry, we've sold out. |
| ほかに何か？ | *hokani naika* | Anything else? |

# menu reader

## GENERAL

| | | |
|---|---|---|
| 一品料理/アラカルト | ippin ryohri /ara karu to | à la carte |
| 朝食 | choh shoku | breakfast |
| モーニングセット | moh ningu setto | set breakfast |
| デザート | dezah to | dessert |
| コーヒー、デザート付き | koh hii, dezahto tsuki | dessert and coffee included |
| 揚げ物 | agemono | deep-fried dishes |
| 夕食/ディナー | yuushoku/dinah | dinner |
| 魚料理 | sakana ryohri | fish dishes |
| 一人前 | ichi nin mae | for one person |
| 二人前 | ni nin mae | for two people |
| 前菜 | zensai | starters |
| おすすめ | osusume | specials |
| …付き | …tsuki | comes with… |
| 軽食 | keishoku | light meals |
| 昼食/ランチ | chuu shoku/ranchi | lunch |
| 肉料理 | niku ryohri | meat dishes |
| サービス料込み | sahbisu ryhoh komi | service included |
| セットメニュー/定食 | setto menyuu /tei shoku | set menu |
| 税込み | zei komi | tax included |
| 税、サービス料込み | zei, sahbisu ryoh komi | tax and service included |
| ケーキセット | keiki setto | tea/coffee plus a choice of cake |
| コーヒーまたは紅茶付き | koh hii matawa koh cha tsuki | tea or coffee included |

## DRINKS

| | | |
|---|---|---|
| ボトル | *botoru* | bottle |
| バーボン | *bah bon* | bourbon |
| ブランデー | *buran deh* | brandy |
| ビール | *biiru* | beer |
| 瓶ビール | *bin biiru* | bottled beer |
| 黒ビール | *kuro biiru* | dark beer |
| 生ビール | *nama biiru* | draught beer |
| シャンペン | *shanpen* | champagne |
| ココア(ホット/アイス) | *koko a (hotto/aisu)* | chocolate (hot/cold) |
| りんご酒 | *ringoshu* | cider |
| カクテル | *kakuteru* | cocktail |
| コーヒー | *koh hii* | coffee |
| ブラック | *burakku* | black |
| カフェイン抜き | *kafein nuki* | decaffeinated |
| アイス | *aisu* | iced |
| ミルク入り | *miruku iri* | white |
| コニャック | *konyakku* | cognac |
| サイダー | *saidah* | fizzy drink |
| 冷たい飲み物 | *tsumetai nomi mono* | iced drink |
| ジン | *jin* | gin |
| ジントニック | *jin tonikku* | gin and tonic |
| お茶 | *ocha* | green tea |
| 氷 | *kohri* | ice |
| アイスコーヒー | *aisu koh hii* | iced coffee |
| アイスティー | *aisu tii* | iced tea |
| ジュース | *juu su* | juice |
| グレープフルーツ | *gureipu furuu tsu* | grapefruit |
| レモン | *remon* | lemon |
| オレンジ | *orenji* | orange |
| パイナップル | *painappuru* | pineapple |
| トマト | *tomato* | tomato |

food and drink

117

| レモネード | remoneido | lemonade |
|---|---|---|
| ミルク(ホット/冷たい) | miruku (hotto/tsumetai) | milk (hot/cold) |
| スパークリングウォーター/炭酸水 | supahkuringu wohtah /tansan sui | (sparkling) mineral water |
| 梅酒 | ume shu | plum wine |
| ラム酒 | ramu shu | rum |
| 日本酒/お酒 | nihon shu/o sake | Japanese rice wine/ sake |
| スコッチウイスキー | sukocchi uisukii | Scotch (whisky) |
| 焼酎 | shoh chuu | distilled (Japanese) spirit |
| ソーダ水 | sohda sui | soda |
| ミルクティー/レモンティー | miruku tii/remon tii | tea with milk/lemon |
| トニックウォーター | tonikku wohtah | tonic water |
| ウォツカ | uokka | vodka |
| ワイン | wain | wine |
| ドライ | dorai | dry |
| ハウスワイン | hausu wain | house wine |
| 赤 | aka | red |
| ロゼ | roze | rosé |
| スパークリングワイン | supahkuringu wain | sparkling wine |
| 甘い | ama i | sweet |
| 白 | shiro | white |
| ウィスキー | uisukii | whisky |
| オンザロック | on za rokku | with ice |
| 水割り | mizu wari | with water |

## GENERAL FOOD

| | | |
|---|---|---|
| りんご | *ringo* | apple |
| アスパラガス | *asuparagasu* | asparagus |
| なす | *nasu* | aubergine |
| アボカド | *abogado* | avocado |
| 小豆 | *azuki* | azuki beans |
| ベーコン | *beikon* | bacon |
| 焼いた | *yaita* | baked |
| 竹の子 | *takenoko* | bamboo shoots |
| バナナ | *banana* | banana |
| もやし | *moyashi* | bean sprouts |
| みそ汁 | *miso shiru* | (Japanese) bean-paste soup |
| 豆 | *mame* | beans |
| 牛肉/ビーフ | *gyuu niku/biifu* | beef |
| ゆでた | *yudeta* | boiled |
| 食パン | *shoku pan* | bread (sliced) |
| ロールパン | *rohru pan* | bread roll |
| そらまめ | *sora mame* | broad beans |
| ごぼう | *goboh* | burdock root |
| バター | *batah* | butter |
| キャベツ | *kyabetsu* | cabbage |
| にんじん | *ninjin* | carrot |
| カリフラワー | *karifurawah* | cauliflower |
| セロリ | *serori* | celery |
| さくらんぼ | *sakuranbo* | cherry |
| 栗 | *kuri* | chestnut |
| 鶏肉/チキン | *tori niku/chikin* | chicken |
| チコリー | *chikorii* | chicory |
| 白菜 | *hakusai* | Chinese cabbage |
| はまぐり | *hamaguri* | clams |

food and drink

119

| | | |
|---|---|---|
| お吸い物 | *osuimono* | clear soup |
| ココナッツ | *kokonattsu* | coconut |
| ズッキーニ | *zukkiini* | courgette |
| かに | *kani* | crab |
| きゅうり | *kyuuri* | cucumber |
| カレー | *karei* | curry |
| 鴨 | *kamo* | duck |
| うなぎ | *unagi* | eel |
| 卵 | *tamago* | eggs |
| ポーチドエッグ | *pohchido eggu* | poached |
| ゆで卵 | *yude tamago* | hard-boiled |
| 半熟卵 | *hanjuku tamago* | soft-boiled |
| スクランブルエッグ | *suku ranburu eggu* | scrambled |
| フィレステーキ | *fire suteiki* | fillet steak |
| 魚 | *sakana* | fish |
| 魚の卵 | *sakana no tamago* | fish eggs |
| 炒めた | *itameta* | fried |
| にんにく | *nin niku* | garlic |
| ぶどう | *budoh* | grapes |
| 枝豆 | *edamame* | green soybeans |
| ハーブ | *hah bu* | herbs |
| はちみつ | *hachi mitsu* | honey |
| わさび | *wasabi* | (Japanese) green horseradish |
| アイスクリーム | *aisukuriimu* | ice-cream |
| 車えび | *kuruma ebi* | king prawn |
| ラム | *ramu* | lamb |
| 赤身 | *akami* | lean meat |
| ねぎ | *negi* | leek |
| レモン | *remon* | lemon |
| レタス | *retasu* | lettuce |
| レバー | *rebah* | liver |

| ロブスター/伊勢えび | robusutah/ise ebi | lobster |
| 地元の | jimoto no | local |
| びわ | biwa | loquat (Oriental pear) |
| れんこん | renkon | lotus root |
| 霜降り | shimo furi | marbled beef |
| マリネ | marine | marinated |
| マヨネーズ | mayoneizu | mayonnaise |
| メロン | meron | melon |
| ひき肉 | hiki niku | minced meat |
| マッシュルーム | masshuruumu | mushroom |
| マスタード/からし | masutahdo/karashi | mustard/Japanese mustard |
| 麺 | men | noodles |
| オムレツ | omuretsu | omelette |
| 玉ねぎ | tamanegi | onion |
| オレンジ | orenji | orange |
| かき | kaki | oysters |
| パセリ | paseri | parsley |
| パスタ | pasuta | pasta |
| 桃 | momo | peach |
| ピーナッツ | piinattsu | peanuts |
| 梨/洋梨 | nashi/yohnashi | pear (Japanese/Western) |
| えんどう豆 | endoh mame | peas |
| こしょう | koshoh | pepper |
| ピーマン/赤ピーマン | piiman/aka pii man | peppers green/red |
| 柿 | kaki | persimmon |
| パイナップル | painappuru | pineapple |
| プラム | puramu | plum |
| 豚肉/ポーク | buta niku/pohku | pork |

food and drink

121

| | | |
|---|---|---|
| じゃがいも | *jagaimo* | potatoes |
| プルーン | *puruun* | prune |
| かぼちゃ | *kabocha* | pumpkin |
| 大根 | *daikon* | (Japanese) radish |
| レーズン | *reizun* | raisins |
| ラズベリー | *razuberii* | raspberry |
| 生/生の | *nama/nama no* | raw |
| 赤キャベツ | *aka kyabetsu* | red cabbage |
| 唐辛子/とうがらし | *toh garashi* | red chilli pepper |
| ばら肉 | *bara niku* | rib |
| 米/ご飯 | *kome/gohan* | uncooked-rice/ steamed rice |
| ロースト | *rohsuto* | roast |
| サラダ | *sarada* | salad |
| 塩 | *shio* | salt |
| サンドイッチ | *sando icchi* | sandwich |
| いわし | *iwashi* | sardines |
| みかん | *mikan* | satsuma |
| ソース | *sohsu* | sauce |
| ソテー | *sotei* | sautéed |
| 帆立貝 | *hotate gai* | scallops |
| シーフード/魚介類 | *shiifuudo/gyokai rui* | seafood |
| 季節の | *kisetsu no* | seasonal |
| しいたけ | *shii take* | shiitake mushroom |
| 串焼き | *kushi yaki* | skewered |
| 燻製 | *kunsei* | smoked |
| シタビラメ | *shitabirame* | sole |
| シャーベット | *shahbetto* | sorbet |
| スープ | *suupu* | soup |
| ほうれん草 | *hoh rensoh* | spinach |
| ステーキ | *suteiki* | steak |
| ご飯/ライス | *gohan/raisu* | steamed rice |

| 煮込んだ | nikonda | stewed |
| イチゴ | ichigo | strawberry |
| さつまいも | satsumaimo | sweet potato |
| とうもろこし/スイートコーン | tohmorokoshi/suiito kohn | sweetcorn |
| トースト | tohsuto | toast |
| とうふ | tofu | tofu |
| にじます | niji masu | trout |
| バニラ | banira | vanilla |
| 子牛の肉 | koushi no niku | veal |
| スイカ | suika | watermelon |
| ヨーグルト | yohguruto | yoghurt |

## JAPANESE SPECIALITIES

| 会席料理 | kaiseki ryohri | Japanese banquet |
| 懐石 | kaiseki | multi-course gourmet meal |
| 茶懐石 | cha kaiseki | light meal associated with tea ceremony |
| 精進料理 | shohjin ryohri | vegetarian meals |
| ちらし鮨 | chirashi zushi | seafood and vegetables/eggs served on a bowl of sushi rice |
| いなり鮨 | inari zushi | fried bean curd stuffed with sushi rice |
| 天ぷら | tenpura | deep-fried battered fish and vegetables |
| 蕎麦 | soba | buckwheat noodles |
| うどん | udon | thick noodles |

| 焼き鳥 | *yakitori* | grilled chicken on skewers |
| とんかつ | *tonkatsu* | pork cutlet |
| 焼肉 | *yakiniku* | do-it-yourself grilled meat |
| ラーメン | *rahmen* | Chinese-style (thin) noodles |
| 牛丼 | *gyuudon* | cooked beef and vegetables served on a bowl of rice |
| すきやき | *sukiyaki* | thinly sliced beef, tofu and vegetables simmered (at the table) in a soy-based broth |
| おでん | *oden* | vegetables and fish cake stew simmered in a fish broth |
| カレーライス | *karei raisu* | Japanese style curry with rice |

## SUSHI/SASHIMI FISH

| | | |
|---|---|---|
| あわび | *awabi* | abalone |
| 赤貝 | *akagai* | ark shell |
| 鱈 | *tara* | cod |
| あなご | *anago* | conger eel |
| ひらめ | *hirame* | flatfish |
| 数の子 | *kazunoko* | herring roe |
| あじ | *aji* | horse mackerel |
| さば | *saba* | mackerel |
| たこ | *tako* | octopus |
| えび | *ebi* | prawn |
| 鮭 | *sake* | salmon |
| いくら | *ikura* | salmon roe |
| ほたて | *hotate* | scallop |
| 鯛 | *tai* | sea bream |
| えび | *ebi* | shrimp |
| いか | *ika* | squid |
| かじき | *kajiki* | swordfish |
| マグロ | *maguro* | tuna |
| トロ | *toro* | fatty tuna |
| 赤身 | *akami* | red fish |
| はまち | *hamachi* | yellowtail |
| すし | *sushi* | sushi |
| 握り鮨 | *nigiri zushi* | 'finger' sushi |
| 押し鮨 | *oshi zushi* | 'pressed' sushi |
| 巻き鮨 | *maki zushi* | sushi wrapped with dried seaweed |
| カッパ巻き | *kappa maki* | cucumber roll |
| 鉄火巻き | *tekka maki* | tuna roll |

food and drink

## JAPANESE CAKES AND SNACKS

| | | |
|---|---|---|
| あんこ | *anko* | *azuki* (bean) jam |
| あんぱん | *anpan* | bread roll filled with *azuki* jam |
| 饅頭 | *manjuu* | bun filled with red bean jam |
| 煎餅 | *senbei* | Japanese rice crackers |
| もち | *mochi* | Japanese rice cakes |
| お汁粉/ぜんざい | *oshiruko/zenzai* | sweet *azuki* bean soup, with rice cake |
| カステラ | *kasutera* | sliced sponge cake |
| 鯛焼き | *taiyaki* | fish-shaped festival cake stuffed with *azuki* jam |
| 羊羹 | *yohkan* | sweet *azuki* bean jelly |

food and drink

# sightseeing
# &activities

# ✳ at the tourist office

There are two types of tourist offices in Japan: TICs (Tourist Information Centres) operated by the government, and i-System, a network of regional tourist office. TICs provide free literature, advice and itinerary planning but do not make bookings.

i-System offices are usually located in railway stations and town centres. They provide detailed information on local tourism, and make bookings.

## YOU MAY WANT TO SAY...

| | | |
|---|---|---|
| Do you speak English? | 英語を話しますか? | *eigo o hanashi mas ka* |
| Do you have...<br>　a map of that town? | …はありますか?<br>　その町の地図 | *...wa ari mas ka*<br>　*sono machi no chizu* |
| 　a list of hotels? | 　ホテルのリスト | 　*hoteru no risuto* |
| Can you recommend a... | …を教えてください? | *...o oshi ete kudasai* |
| 　cheap hotel?<br>　good campsite? | 　安いホテル<br>　良いキャンプ場 | 　*yasui hoteru*<br>　*ii kyanpu joh* |
| 　traditional restaurant? | 　日本的な料理店? | 　*nihon teki na ryohri ten* |
| Do you have information...<br>　in English? | …案内はありますか?<br>　英語の | *...annai wa arimas ka*<br>　*Eigo no* |
| 　about opening times? | 　営業時間の | 　*eigyoh jikan no* |

sightseeing and activities

128

| | | |
|---|---|---|
| Can you book... | …を予約してもらえ ますか？ | ...o yoyaku shite morae mas ka |
| a hotel room for me? | ホテルの部屋 | hoteru no heya |
| this day-trip for me? | この日帰り旅行 | kono higaeri ryokoh |
| Where is... | …はどこですか？ | ...wa doko des ka |
| the Imperial Palace? | 皇居 | koh kyo |
| the art gallery? | 美術館 | bijutsukan |
| the... museum? | …博物館 | ...hakubutsukan |
| Is there a post office near here? | この近くに郵便局は ありますか？ | kono chikaku ni yuubink yoku wa arimas ka |
| Could you show me on the map? | この地図で教えてい ただけますか？ | kono chizu de oshi ete itadake mas ka |

## * opening times
(see **telling the time**, page 20)

● Shops generally open from 10am to 8pm, attractions from 9am. Small shops catering to tourists are open every day, department stores close one weekday each week.

### YOU MAY WANT TO SAY...

| | | |
|---|---|---|
| What time does the... close? | …は, 何時に閉まり ますか？ | ...wa, nan ji ni shimari mas ka |
| When does the... open? | …は, 何時からで すか？ | ...wa, nan ji kara des ka |

sightseeing and activities

129

- **Is it open...**
  **on Mondays?**
  **on weekends?**

…は開いていますか？
月曜日
週末

*...wa aite imas ka*
*getsu yoh bi*
*shuu matsu*

- **Is it open to the public?**

それは一般に公開されていますか？

*sore wa ippan ni koh kai sarete imas ka*

## YOU MAY HEAR...

| …以外は毎日開いています。 | *...igai wa mai nichi aite imas* | It's open every day except... |
| …から…まで開いています。 | *...kara ...made aite imas* | It's open from... to... |
| 閉まっています。 | *shimatte imas* | It's closed. |
| 冬/夏は閉まっています。 | *fuyu/natsu wa shimatte imas* | It's closed in winter/summer. |
| 改装のため閉まっています。 | *kaisoh no tame shimatte imas* | It's closed for renovation. |

# * visiting places

## YOU MAY SEE...

| 券売機 | *ken bai ki* | automatic ticket machine |
| クローク | *kuroh ku* | cloakroom |
| 閉館/閉店 | *heikan/heiten* | closed |
| 立入禁止 | *tachi iri kin shi* | no entry |
| 触らないで下さい | *sawara nai de kudasai* | do not touch |
| 非常口 | *hijoh guchi* | emergency exit |
| 入口 | *iri guchi* | entrance |

| | | |
|---|---|---|
| 出口 | *de guchi* | **exit** |
| 料金 | *ryoh kin* | **fee** |
| 無料 | *muryoh* | **free (of charge)** |
| 入場無料 | *nyuu joh muryoh* | **free admission** |
| ガイド付きツアー | *gaido tsuki tsuah* | **guided tours** |
| 芝生立入禁止 | *shibafu tachi iri kin shi* | **keep off the grass** |
| 静かに | *shizuka ni* | **keep quiet** |
| 手荷物預かり所 | *tenimotsu azu kari sho* | **left-luggage** |
| エレベーター | *erebeh tah* | **lift** |
| ロッカー | *rokkah* | **locker** |
| 立入禁止 | *tachi iri kin shi* | **no entry** |
| フラッシュ禁止 | *furasshu kin shi* | **no flash photography** |
| 駐車禁止 | *chuu sha kin shi* | **no parking** |
| 撮影禁止 | *satsuei kin shi* | **no photography** |
| 禁煙 | *kinen* | **no smoking** |
| 開館/営業中 | *kai kan/eigyoh chuu* | **open** |
| 開館時間/営業時間 | *kai kan jikan/eigyoh jikan* | **opening hours** |
| 駐車場 | *chusha joh* | **parking** |
| 関係者以外立入禁止 | *kankei sha igai tachi iri kin shi* | **private** |
| 順路 | *junro* | **route** |
| 土産物店 | *miyagemono ten* | **souvenir shop** |
| 階段 | *kaidan* | **stairs** |
| 電話 | *denwa* | **telephone** |
| チケット売場 | *chiketto uriba* | **ticket office** |
| 団体/グループ | *dantai/guruupu* | **tour group** |
| 車椅子 | *kuruma isu* | **wheelchair** |

sightseeing and activities

## YOU MAY WANT TO SAY...

| | | |
|---|---|---|
| How much does it cost? | いくらですか? | *ikura des ka* |
| One adult, please. | 大人 一枚，お願いします。 | *otona ichimai, onegai shimas* |
| Two adults, please. | 大人 二枚，お願いします。 | *otona nimai, onegai shimas* |
| One adult and two children, please. | 大人一枚と子供二枚，お願いします。 | *otona ichimai to kodomo nimai onegai shimas* |
| Is there a discount for... | …割引はありますか? | *...wari biki wa ari mas ka* |
| students? | 学生 | *gakusei* |
| senior citizens? | 高齢者の | *kohreisha no* |
| children? | 子供の | *kodomo no* |
| the disabled? | 障害者の | *shougaisha no* |
| Is there wheelchair access? | 車椅子が使えますか? | *kurumaisu ga tsukae mas ka* |
| Is there... | …はありますか? | *...wa ari mas ka* |
| an audio-tour? | 音声ガイド | *onsei gaido* |
| a picnic area? | ピクニックができるところ | *piku nikku ga dekiru tokoro* |
| Are there guided tours (in English)? | 英語を話すガイドのツアーはありますか? | *eigo o hanasu gaido no tsuah wa arimas ka* |
| Can I take photos? | 写真を撮ってもいいですか? | *shashin o tottemo ii des ka* |
| Could you take our photo, please? | 私たちの写真を撮っていただけますか? | *watashi tachi no shashin o totte itadake mas ka* |

| When was this built? | これはいつ建てられましたか? | kore wa itsu taterare mashita ka |
| Who painted that? | あれを描いたのは誰ですか? | are o kaita nowa dare des ka |

## YOU MAY HEAR...

| 一人千円です。 | hitori sen en des | It costs ¥1,000 per person. |
| …割引がございます<br>　学生<br>　高齢者の | …waribiki ga gozai mas<br>gakusei<br>koh rei sha no | There's a discount for…<br>students<br>senior citizens |
| お子さんは何歳ですか? | okosan wa nansai des ka | How old is/are your children? |
| 十二歳以下の子供は無料です。 | juu ni sai ika no kodomo wa muryoh des | Children under 12 go free. |
| 車椅子用のスロープがあります。 | kuruma isu yoh no surohpu ga arimas | There are wheelchair ramps. |
| 申し訳ございませんが, 車椅子はちょっと難しいです。 | moh shi wake gozai masen ga, kuruma isu wa chotto muzukashii des | I'm sorry, it's not suitable for wheelchairs. |
| ツアーに参加しませんか? | tsuah ni sanka shimasen ka | Would you like to join a tour? |
| 音声ガイドは五百円です。 | onsei gaido wa go hyaku en des | The audio-tour costs ¥500. |
| この画家/建築家は… | kono gaka/kenchiku ka wa … | The painter/ architect was… |

sightseeing and activities

133

| 明治時代に建てられました。 | *meiji jidai ni tate rare mashita* | It was built in the Meiji era. |
| …に描かれました 昭和初期 | *…ni egakare mashita shouwa shoki* | It was painted in… the early Showa era |
| 1912年 | *sen kyuu hyaku juu ni nen* | 1912 |
| 80年代 | *hachi juu nen dai* | the Eighties |

## ✳ going on tours and trips

### YOU MAY WANT TO SAY…

| I/We'd like to join the tour to… | …のツアーに参加したいんですが。 | *…no tsuah ni san ka shitain des ga* |
| What time does it… | …は何時ですか？ | *…wa nan ji des ka* |
|   leave? | 出発 | *shuppatsu* |
|   get back? | 帰り | *kaeri* |
| How long is it? | どのくらいかかりますか？ | *dono kurai kakari mas ka* |
| Where does it leave from? | どこから出発しますか？ | *doko kara shuppatsu shimas ka* |
| Does the guide speak English? | ガイドの方は英語を話しますか？ | *gaido no kata wa eigo o hanashi mas ka* |
| How much is it? | いくらかかりますか？ | *ikura kakari mas ka* |
| Is… included? | …は含まれていますか？ | *…wa fukumarete imas ka* |
|   lunch | 昼食/ランチ | *chuushoku/ranchi* |
|   accommodation | 宿泊 | *shuku haku* |

sightseeing and activities

| | | |
|---|---|---|
| **When's the next...** | 次の … はいつで<br>すか? | *tsugi no ... wa itsu*<br>*des ka* |
| pleasure boat<br>trip?<br>day-trip? | 遊覧船<br>日帰り旅行 | *yuu ran sen*<br>*higaeri ryokoh* |
| **Can we hire an<br>(English-speaking)<br>guide?** | 英語を話すガイドの<br>方をお願いできま<br>すか。 | *eigo o hanasu gaido*<br>*no kata o onegai*<br>*dekimas ka* |
| **I/We'd like to see...** | …が見たいんです<br>が。 | *...ga mita in des ga* |
| **I'm with a (tour)<br>group.** | 団体/グループで来<br>ています。 | *dantai/guruupu de*<br>*kite imas* |
| **I've lost my (tour)<br>group.** | グループから離れて<br>しまいました。 | *guruupu kara hana*<br>*rete shimai mashita* |

## YOU MAY HEAR...

| | | |
|---|---|---|
| 入口に集合して下<br>さい。 | *iri guchi ni shuugoh*<br>*shite kudasai* | **Please meet at the<br>entrance.** |
| …に出発します。 | *...ni shuppatsu shimas* | **It leaves at...** |
| …に戻ります。 | *...ni modori mas* | **It gets back at...** |
| …から出発しま<br>す。 | *...kara shuppatsu*<br>*shimas* | **It leaves from...** |
| 遅れないで下さ<br>い。 | *okure naide kudasai* | **Don't be late!** |
| 料金は一日 … で<br>す。 | *ryohkin wa ichi nichi*<br>*... des* | **The charge is ... per<br>day.** |
| グループの名前は<br>何ですか? | *guruupu no namae*<br>*wa nan des ka* | **What's the name of<br>your group?** |

sightseeing and activities

135

# ✱ tourist glossary

## YOU MAY SEE...

| | | |
|---|---|---|
| 遊園地/テーマパーク | *yuu en chi/teíma pahku* | amusement/theme park |
| 水族館 | *suizokkan* | aquarium |
| 美術館 | *bijutsu kan* | art gallery |
| 橋 | *hashi* | bridge |
| 城 | *shiro* | castle |
| 天皇 | *ten noh* | emperor |
| 皇后 | *koh goh* | empress |
| 時代 | *jidai* | era |
| 展覧会/博覧会 | *tenran kai/hakuran kai* | exhibition |
| 庭園 | *tei en* | gardens |
| 温泉 | *onsen* | hot spring/spa |
| 皇居 | *koh kyo* | Imperial Palace |
| 記念碑/遺跡 | *kinenhi/iseki* | monument |
| 博物館 | *hakubutsukan* | museum |
| 公園 | *kohen* | park |
| 神社 | *jinja* | shrine |
| おみやげ | *omiyage* | souvenir |
| 広場 | *hiroba* | square |
| スタジアム/球場 | *sutajiamu/kyuu joh* | stadium |
| 寺/寺院 | *tera/ji in* | temple |
| 劇場 | *geki joh* | theatre |
| 火山 | *kazan* | volcano |
| 世界遺産 | *sekai isan* | world heritage |
| 動物園 | *dohbutsu en* | zoo |

# ✳ entertainment

● Japan offers every conceivable type of entertainment, from traditional, uniquely Japanese, e.g. *sumo* (相撲), *karaoke* (カラオケ), *taiko* drumming, to contemporary sports and international theatre and musical tours.

## YOU MAY SEE...

| | | |
|---|---|---|
| バレエ | *bareh* | ballet |
| ボックス席 | *bokkusu seki* | boxes |
| 映画館 | *eigakan* | cinema |
| コンサートホール | *konsahto hohru* | concert hall |
| ディスコ | *disuko* | discotheque |
| 夜の部 | *yoru no bu* | evening performance |
| 出口 | *deguchi* | exit |
| ナイトクラブ | *naito kurabu* | nightclub |
| オーケストラ | *oh kesutora* | orchestra |
| 列 | *retsu* | row |
| 売切れ | *urikire* | sold out |
| スタジアム/球場 | *sutajiamu/kyuu joh* | stadium |
| 劇場 | *geki joh* | theatre |
| 開演中は入場をご遠慮下さい。 | *kai en chuu wa nyuu joh o goen ryoh kudasai* | no entry once the performance has begun. |
| 十八歳未満お断り | *juu hassai miman okoto wari* | over-18s only |
| 吹き替え映画 | *fuki kae eiga* | Japanese-dubbed (foreign film) |
| 歌舞伎 | *kabuki* | kabuki |
| カラオケ | *karaoke* | karaoke |

| | | |
|---|---|---|
| 自由席 | *jiyuu seki* | **non-reserved seat** |
| 延期 | *enki* | **postponed** |
| プログラム | *puroguramu* | **programme** |
| 払い戻し | *harai modoshi* | **refund** |
| 指定席 | *shiteiseki* | **reserved seat** |
| 空席あり | *kuu seki ari* | **seats available** |
| 完売 | *kan bai* | **sold out** |
| 相撲 | *sumou* | **sumo** |
| 茶道 | *sadoh* | **tea ceremony** |

## YOU MAY WANT TO SAY...

- **What is there to do in the evenings here?** ここでは夕方に何が行われますか？ *koko dewa yuugata ni nani ga oko naware mas ka*

- **Is there anything for children?** 子供向けのものはありますか？ *kodomo muke no mono wa arimas ka*

- **Is there ... around here?** この辺に … がありますか？ *konohen ni ... ga ari mas ka*
    - **a cinema** 映画館 *eigakan*
    - **a good nightclub** いいクラブ *ii kurabu*

- **What's on...** …何をやっていますか？ *...nani o yatte imas ka*

    - **tonight?** 今晩は *konban wa*
    - **tomorrow?** 明日は *ashita wa*
    - **at the theatre?** この劇場では *kono geki joh dewa*
    - **at the cinema?** この映画館では *kono eiga kan dewa*

sightseeing and activities

138

| Is there a football match this weekend? | 今週末，サッカーの試合がありますか? | kon shuu matsu, sakkah no shiai ga arimas ka |
| When does the... begin? | …はいつ始まりますか? | ...wa itsu haji mari mas ka |
| game | 試合 | shiai |
| performance | 公演 | kohen |
| What time does it finish? | 何時に終わりますか? | nanji ni owari mas ka |
| How long is it? | どのくらいかかりますか | dono kurai kakari mas ka |
| Do we need to book? | 予約は必要ですか? | yoyaku wa hitsuyoh des ka |
| Where can I get tickets? | どこでチケットが買えますか? | doko de chiketto ga kae mas ka |
| Is it suitable for children? | それは子供向けですか? | sore wa kodomo muke des ka |
| Has the film got English subtitles? | その映画に英語の字幕がありますか。 | sono eiga ni eigo no jimaku ga arimas ka |
| Is it dubbed? | 吹き替えですか? | fuki kae des ka |
| Who's... | 誰が… ですか? | dare ga... des ka |
| singing? | 歌っているん | utatte iru n |
| playing? | 演奏しているん | ensou shite irun |
| in that? | 出ているん | dete iru n |

sightseeing and activities

**YOU MAY HEAR...**

| …に始まります。 | ...ni haji mari mas | It starts at... |
| …に終わります。 | ...ni owari mas | It finishes at... |

## booking tickets

| 約 … かかります | yaku … kakari mas | It lasts about… |
| 二時間 | ni jikan | two hours |
| 一時間半 | ichi jikan han | an hour and a half |

| 事前に予約するのが一番良いと思います。 | jizen ni yoyaku suru noga ichi ban ii to omoi mas | It's best to book in advance. |

| 吹き替えです。 | fuki kae des | It's dubbed. |

| 日本語の字幕付きです。 | nihon go no jimaku tsuki des | It's got Japanese subtitles. |

| ここでチケットが買えます。 | koko de chiketto ga kae mas | You can buy tickets here. |

# ✳ booking tickets

### YOU MAY WANT TO SAY...

| Can you get me tickets for… | …のチケットがほしいんですが? | …no chiketto ga hoshi in des ga |
| the ballet? | バレエ | bareh |
| the kabuki performance? | 歌舞伎 | kabuki |
| the sumo (tournament)? | 相撲 | sumou |

| Are there any seats left for Saturday? | 土曜日の席はまだありますか? | doyoh bi no seki wa mada ari mas ka |

| I'd like to book… | …の予約をしたいんですが | …no yoyaku o shita in des ga |
| a box | ボックス席 | bokkusu seki |
| two seats | 二人分 | futari bun |

- **Do you have anything cheaper?** もう少し安いものはありますか? *moh sukoshi yasuimono wa arimas ka*

- **Is there wheelchair access?** 車椅子が使えますか? *kuruma isu ga tsukae mas ka*

## YOU MAY HEAR...

- 何名様ですか? *nan mei sama des ka* **For how many people?**

- いつですか? *itsu des ka* **When for?**

- クレジットカードはありますか? *kurejitto kahdo wa arimas ka* **Do you have a credit card?**

- 申し訳ありませんが, その日/夜の部は売り切れました。 *mohshi wake ari masenga, sono hi/yoru no bu wa uri kire mashita* **I'm sorry we're sold out that day/night.**

## ✳ at the show

### YOU MAY WANT TO SAY...

- **What... is on tonight?**
  film
  play
  今夜, 何の…がありますか?
  映画
  芝居
  *konya nan no ... ga arimas ka*
  *eiga*
  *shibai*

- **Two for tonight's performance, please.** 今夜のチケットを二枚, お願いします。 *konya no chiketto o nimai onegai shimas*

*sightseeing and activities*

141

## at the show

| One adult and two children, please. | 大人一人と子供二人お願いします。 | *otona hitori to kodomo futari, onegai shimas* |
| How much is that? | それはいくらですか? | *sore wa ikura des ka* |
| We'd like to sit... | …に座りたいんですが | *...ni suwaritain des ga* |
| at the front | 前の方 | *mae no hoh* |
| at the back | 後の方 | *ushiro no hoh* |
| in the middle | 真ん中の席 | *mannaka no seki* |
| We've reserved seats. | 席を予約しています。 | *seki o yoyaku shite imas* |
| Is there an interval? | 休憩はありますか。 | *kyuukei wa arimas ka* |
| Where are the toilets? | トイレはどこですか。 | *toire wa doko des ka* |

### YOU MAY HEAR...

| クレジットカードを拝見させて下さい。 | *kure jitto kahdo o haiken sasete kudasai* | May I have your credit card, please? |
| 申し訳ありませんが, 今夜は満席です。 | *mohshi wake ari masen ga, konya wa manseki des* | Sorry, we're full tonight. |
| どちらの席がよろしいですか? | *dochira no seki ga yoroshii des ka* | Where would you like to sit? |
| プログラムはいかがですか? | *puro guramu wa ikaga des ka* | Would you like a programme? |

sightseeing and activities

# * sports and activities

● Japan's most popular sports are fishing, golf and baseball. Japanese ski resorts are often based near natural thermal spas - *onsen* (温泉), some have outdoor *onsen* - *rotenburo* (露天風呂).

● Climbing and rambling are popular. Mt. Fuji, Japan's highest peak, is open to climbers in July and August. 10% of the world's volcanoes are in Japan, and some are still active.

## YOU MAY SEE...

| | | |
|---|---|---|
| 野球 | *yakyuu* | baseball |
| バスケットボール | *basuketto bohru* | basketball |
| 海岸 | *kaigan* | beach |
| 貸しボート | *kashi bohto* | boat hire |
| ケーブルカー | *keiburu kah* | cable car |
| リフト | *rifuto* | chair lift |
| 危険 | *kiken* | danger |
| 応急手当 | *ohkyuu teate* | first aid |
| サッカー | *sakkah* | football |
| サッカー競技場 | *sakkah kyougi joh* | football pitch |
| 試合 | *shiai* | game |
| ゴール | *gohru* | goal |
| ゴルフ | *gorufu* | golf |
| ゴルフコース | *gorufu koh su* | golf course |
| ハイキング | *haikingu* | hiking |
| ジョギング | *jogingu* | jogging |
| 遊泳禁止 | *yuuei kinshi* | no swimming |
| レンタルスキー | *rentaru skii* | ski hire |
| リフト | *rifuto* | ski lift |

143

## sports and activities

| | | |
|---|---|---|
| スキースクール | *skii sukuuru* | ski school |
| スキー場 | *skii jyoh* | ski slope |
| スノーボード | *sunoh bohdo* | snowboard |
| スポーツセンター | *supohtsu sentah* | sports centre |
| スカッシュ | *sukasshu* | squash |
| 水泳 | *suiei* | swimming |
| 屋内プール | *okunai puuru* | swimming pool (indoor) |
| 屋外プール | *okugai puuru* | swimming pool (outdoor) |
| テニスコート | *tenisu kohto* | tennis court |
| バレーボール | *bareh bohru* | volleyball |
| ヨガ | *yoga* | yoga |

### YOU MAY WANT TO SAY...

- **Where can I try/observe ...** どこで…が出来ま/すか？ *doko de ... ga deki mas ka*
  - **flower arrangement?** 生け花 *ikebana*
  - **tea ceremony?** 茶道 *sadoh*
  - **cherry-blossom viewing?** 花見 *hanami*

- **Could I/we...** …が出来ますか？ *...ga deki mas ka*
  - **climb Mt. Fuji?** 富士登山 *fuji tozan*
  - **try calligraphy?** 書道 *shodoh*

- **I'm...** 私は … です *watashi wa ... des*
  - **a beginner** 初心者 *shoshin sha*
  - **quite experienced** 上級者 *johkyuu sha*

- **How much does it cost...** …いくらですか? *...ikura des ka*
  - **per hour?** 一時間 *ichi jikan*
  - **per day?** 一日 *ichi nichi*
  - **per week?** 一週間 *isshuu kan*

- **Can I/we hire...** …を借りることが出来ますか? *...o kariru koto ga deki mas ka*
  - **clubs?** クラブ *kurabu*
  - **racquets?** ラケット *raketto*

- **Do I/we have to be a member?** メンバーでなければなりませんか? *menbah de nakereba nari masen ka*

- **Is there a discount for children?** 子供の割引はありますか? *kodomo no waribiki wa ari mas ka*

## YOU MAY HEAR...

| | | |
|---|---|---|
| 初心者ですか? | *shoshin sha des ka* | Are you a beginner? |
| 一時間三千円です。 | *ichi jikan sanzen en des* | It costs ¥3,000 per hour. |
| 予約でいっぱいです。 | *yoyaku de ippai des* | We're fully-booked. |
| また後で来てください。 | *mata atode kite kudasai* | Come back later, please. |
| 明日は空きがあります。 | *ashita wa aki ga arimas* | We've got places tomorrow. |
| サイズはいくつですか? | *saizu wa ikutsu des ka* | What size are you? |

## ✳ at the beach, lake or river

### YOU MAY WANT TO SAY...

- **May I/we...**
  …で泳ぐことが出来ますか？ ここ
  *...de oyogu koto ga dekimas ka*

  **swim here?**
  *koko*

- **Is it safe for children?**
  子供に安全ですか？
  *kodomo ni anzen des ka*

- **When is high tide?**
  満潮はいつですか？
  *manchoh wa itsu des ka*

- **Is the water clean?**
  水はきれいですか？
  *mizu wa kirei des ka*

- **Where is the lifeguard?**
  監視員はどこにいますか？
  *kanshi in wa doko ni imas ka*

### YOU MAY HEAR...

| | | |
|---|---|---|
| 気をつけて下さい。 | *ki o tsukete kudasai* | Be careful. |
| 危険です。 | *kiken des* | It's dangerous. |
| 台風が近づいています。 | *taifuu ga chika zuite imas* | A typhoon is coming. |

### YOU MAY SEE...

| | | |
|---|---|---|
| 飛び込み禁止 | *tobikomi kinshi* | No diving |
| 走るな | *hashiru na* | No running |
| この先 危険 | *konosaki kiken* | Danger, beyond this point. |
| 遊泳禁止 | *yuuei kinshi* | Swimming is not permitted. |

# shops&services

# ✳ shopping

● Department stores *(depahto)* are often conveniently located near main stations. Many also have galleries, restaurants, foreign exchange facilities and basement gourmet food halls.

## YOU MAY SEE...

| | | |
|---|---|---|
| 骨董品 | *kottoh hin* | antiques |
| ベーカリー | *beikarii* | bakery |
| 地階/B | *chikai* | basement |
| 　地下一階/B1F | *chika ikkai* | b1 (sub-level 1) |
| 　地下二階/B2F | *chika nikai* | b2 (sub-level 2) |
| 本屋/書店 | *hon ya/sho ten* | bookshop |
| 洋菓子店 | *yoh gashi ten* | cake shop |
| レジ/会計 | *reji/kaikei* | cashier |
| 試着室 | *shichaku shitsu* | changing room |
| 薬局 | *yakkyoku* | chemist |
| 閉店/休業中 | *heiten/kyuu gyoh chuu* | closed |
| 衣料品/衣類 | *iryoh hin /irui* | clothing |
| コンピューター | *kon pyuu tah* | computers |
| 和菓子屋 | *wagashi ya* | confectioner (Japanese) |
| デパート/百貨店 | *depahto/hyakka ten* | department store |
| 安売り | *yasu uri* | discount |
| 触れないで下さい | *furenai de kudasai* | do not touch |
| クリーニング店/ドライクリーニング | *kuriiningu ten /dorai kuriiningu* | dry cleaner |
| 電気製品 | *denki seihin* | electrical goods |

| | | |
|---|---|---|
| 非常口 | *hijoh guchi* | emergency exit |
| エレベーター | *erebeitah* | elevator |
| 入口 | *iri guchi* | entrance |
| エスカレーター | *esukareitah* | escalator |
| 二階/2F | *nikai* | first floor (UK) |
| 魚屋 | *sakana ya* | fishmonger |
| ご案内/フロアガイド | *goannai/furoa gaido* | floor plan/store directory |
| 食品 | *shoku hin* | foodstuffs |
| 履物/靴 | *haki mono/kutsu* | footwear |
| ギフト/贈り物 | *gifuto/okuri mono* | gifts |
| 一階/1F | *ikkai* | ground floor (UK) |
| 八百屋 | *yaoya* | greengrocer |
| 美容室 | *biyoh shitsu* | hairdresser |
| 健康食品 | *kenkoh shokuhin* | health foods |
| 呉服 | *gofuku* | kimonos |
| 眼鏡/メガネ店 | *megane/megane ten* | optician |
| 香水 | *kohsui* | perfumery |
| 写真 | *shashin* | photography |
| 郵便局/〒 | *yuubin kyoku* | post office |
| 値下げ | *nesage* | reduced |
| 靴屋 | *kutsuya* | shoe shop |
| ショッピングセンター | *shoppingu sentah* | shopping centre |
| 喫煙所/室 | *kitsuen jo/shitsu* | smoking area/room |
| みやげ物 | *miyage mono* | souvenirs |
| スポーツ用品 | *supohtsu yohhin* | sports goods |
| 文房具店 | *bunbohgu ten* | stationer |
| スーパー | *suupah* | supermarket |
| おもちゃ屋/玩具店 | *omocha ya/gangu ten* | toy shop |

- **Where is...**
  **the shopping centre?**
  **the post office?**

  …はどこですか？
  ショッピングセンター
  郵便局

  *...wa doko des ka*
  *shoppingu sentah*

  *yuubin kyoku*

- **Where can I buy...**

  **suntan lotion?**
  **a map?**

  …はどこで買えますか？
  日焼けローション
  地図

  *...wa doko de kae mas ka*
  *hiyake rohshon*
  *chizu*

- **I'd like ..., please.**
  **this one here**
  **that one there**
  **two of those**

  …お願いします。
  これを
  それを
  それを二つ

  *...onegai shimas*
  *kore o*
  *sore o*
  *sore o futatsu*

- **Have you got...?**

  …はありますか？

  *...wa ari mas ka*

- **How much does/ do it/they cost?**

  それはいくらですか？

  *sore wa ikura des ka*

- **Could you write it down, please?**

  それを紙に書いていただけませんか？

  *sore o kami ni kaite itadake masen ka*

- **I'm just browsing.**

  見ているだけです。

  *mite iru dake des*

- **There's one over there, on display.**

  あそこに飾ってあります。

  *asoko ni kazatte arimas*

- **I'll take it.**

  それにします。／それをお願いします。

  *sore ni shimas/sore o onegai shimas*

- **Does it come with a guarantee?**

  保証書は付いてますか？

  *hoshoh sho wa tsuite imas ka*

- **I'd like to think about it.**

  ちょっと考えさせて下さい。

  *chotto kangae sasete kudasai*

- Could you...
    keep it for me?
    order it/some
    for me?

  …もらえませんか?
  取っておいて
  注文して

  ...morae masen ka
  totte oite
  chuumon shite

- Thanks, that's all.   それで全部です。   sorede zenbu des

## YOU MAY HEAR...

| | | |
|---|---|---|
| いらっしゃいませ | irasshai ma se | May I help you? |
| 三千八百円です。 | san zen happyaku en des | It costs ¥3,800. |
| こちらはいかがですか。 | kochira wa ikaga des ka? | How about this one? |
| 申し訳ございませんが，売り切れました | moh shiwake gozai masen ga, uri kire mashita | I'm sorry, we've sold out. |
| 注文できますが。 | chuumon deki mas ga | We can order it for you. |
| 在庫を調べて参ります。 | zaiko o shirabete mairi mas | I'll check to see if we have one/some in stock. |
| どうもありがとうございました。また，お越し下さいませ。 | dohmo arigatoh gozai mashita. Mata okoshi kudasai mase. | Thank you very much. Please come again. |

# * paying

## YOU MAY WANT TO SAY...

- **Where do I pay?** レジはどこですか？ *regii wa doko des ka*
- **Do you accept credit cards?** クレジットカードは使えますか？ *kurejitto kahdo wa tsukae mas ka*
- **Could you wrap it, please?** 包装して下さい。 *hohsoh shite kudasai*
- **May I have... please?** …をいただけますか？ *...o itadake mas ka*
  - a receipt レシート *reshiito*
  - a bag 袋 *fukuro*

## YOU MAY HEAR...

| 贈り物ですか？ | *okuri mono des ka* | Is it a gift? |
| プレゼント用に包装致しましょうか？ | *purezento yoh ni hohsoh itashi mashoh ka* | Would you like it gift-wrapped? |
| 袋はご入り用ですか？ | *fukuro wa goiri yoh des ka* | Would you like a bag? |
| お支払いはどのようになさいますか？ | *oshiharai wa dono yoh ni nasai mas ka* | How would you like to pay? |
| …を拝見させて下さい | *...o haiken sasete kudasai* | May I see... please? |
| 身分証明書 | *mibun shoumei sho* | some ID |
| パスポート | *pasuphohto* | your passport |

## ✳ buying clothes and shoes

(see **clothes and shoe sizes** page 25)

(see **clothes and shoe sizes** page 25)

### YOU MAY WANT TO SAY...

| | | |
|---|---|---|
| Have you got... | …はありますか? | ...wa arimas ka |
| a smaller size? | もっと小さいサイズ | motto chiisai saizu |
| a larger size? | もっと大きいサイズ | motto ohkii saizu |
| other colours? | 別の色 | betsuno iro |
| I'm looking for... | …を探しているんですが | ...o sagashite iru n des ga |
| a hat | 帽子 | bohshi |
| a jumper | セーター | sehtah |
| kimono | 着物 | kimono |
| a shirt | ワイシャツ | wai shatsu |
| A pair of sandals. | サンダル | sandaru |
| A pair of trousers. | ズボン | zubon |
| Where are the changing rooms? | 試着室はどこですか? | shichaku shitsu wa doko des ka |

## ✳ changing rooms

### YOU MAY WANT TO SAY...

| | | |
|---|---|---|
| May I try this on, please? | これを着てみてもいいですか? | kore o kite mite mo ii des ka |
| This doesn't fit. | これは合いません。 | kore wa aimasen |
| It's too... | …すぎます | ...sugi mas |
| big | 大き | ohki |
| small | 小さ | chiisa |
| It doesn't suit me. | 私には似合いません。 | watashi niwa niai masen |

shops and services

153

## exchanges and refunds

| | | |
|---|---|---|
| ご試着なさいますか? | goshichaku nasai mas ka | Would you like to try it/them on? |
| サイズはおいくつですか。 | saizu wa oikutsu des ka? | What size are you? |
| 別のものをお持ちします。 | betsuno mono o omochi shi mas | I'll get you another one. |
| 申し訳ございませんが，それが最後になります。 | mohshi wake gozai masen ga, sore ga saigo ni nari mas | Sorry, that's the last one. |
| お客様にお似合いです。 | okyaku sama ni oniai des | It suits/they suit you. |

## * exchanges and refunds

YOU MAY WANT TO SAY...

| | | |
|---|---|---|
| Excuse me, ...<br>this doesn't work<br>this doesn't fit | すみませんが，…<br>これは壊れています<br>これは合いません | sumimasen ga,<br>kore wa kowarete imas<br>kore wa aimasen |
| I'd like...<br><br>a refund<br>a new one | …をお願いしたいんですが…<br><br>払い戻し<br>新しいのと交換 | ... o onegai shitain des ga<br>harai modoshi<br>atarashii noto kohkan |
| I'd like...<br>to return this<br>to exchange this | …したいんですが…<br>これを返品<br>これを交換 | ...shitain des ga...<br>kore o henpin<br>kore o kohkan |

shops and services

## YOU MAY HEAR...

| | | |
|---|---|---|
| …はお持ちですか？<br>レシート<br>保証書 | …wa omochi des ka<br>reshiito<br>hoshou sho | Do you have...<br>the receipt?<br>the guarantee? |
| 申し訳ございませ<br>んが，レシートが<br>ないと払い戻しは<br>できません。 | mohshi wake gozai<br>masen ga, reshiito ga<br>nai to harai modoshi<br>wa dekimasen | Sorry, we don't give<br>refunds without a<br>receipt. |

## ✳ at the drugstore

(see **at the chemist's**, page 168)

## YOU MAY WANT TO SAY...

| | | |
|---|---|---|
| I need...<br>sanitary towels<br>shampoo<br>shower gel<br>tampons<br>toothpaste | …が欲しいんですが<br>生理用ナプキン<br>シャンプー<br>ボディーソープ<br>タンポン<br>歯磨き粉 | …ga hoshiin des ga<br>seiri yoh napukin<br>shanpuu<br>bodii soupu<br>tanpon<br>hamigaki ko |
| I am looking for... | …を探しているん<br>ですが | …o sagashite irun<br>des ga |
| moisturiser<br>vitamins | ハンドクリーム<br>ビタミン剤 | hando kuriimu<br>bitamin zai |
| I'd like some...<br>make-up<br>remover | …が欲しいんですが<br>メイク落とし | …ga hoshi in des ga<br>meiku otoshi |
| toner<br>foundation | 化粧水<br>ファンデーション | keshoh sui<br>fandeishon |

## ✳ photography

### YOU MAY WANT TO SAY...

- **Can you print photos from a memory card?**
  メモリーカードから写真をプリント出来ますか?
  *memorii kahdo kara shashin o purinto deki mas ka?*

- **When will it/they be ready?**
  いつできますか?
  *itsu dekimas ka*

- **Do you offer an express service?**
  特急サービスがありますか?
  *tokkyuu sahbisu ga arimas ka*

- **How much is it per ...**
  ...は一枚いくらですか?
  *...wa ichimai ikura des ka*
    print?
      プリント
      *purinto*

- **I'd like..., please**
  ...が欲しいんですが
  *...ga hoshi in des ga*
    a 2GB memory card
      2ギガバイトのメモリーカード
      *ni giga baito no memorii kahdo*

- **Do you do repairs?**
  修理は出来ますか?
  *shuuri wa deki mas ka*

### YOU MAY HEAR...

- プリントのサイズはどれがよろしいですか?
  *purinto no saizu wa dore ga yoroshii des ka*
  **What size prints would you like?**

- ...には出来ています
  *...niwa dekite imas*
  **They'll be ready ...**
    明日
      *ashita*
      **tomorrow**
    一時間後
      *ichi jikan go*
      **in an hour**

# ✳ at the convenience store

● Convenience stores *konbini* (コンビニ) sell a variety of snacks and drinks, and they also have cash machines, microwave facilities (used to heat up snacks bought on the premises) and luggage delivery services 宅配便 *(takuhaibin)*. Delivery companies transport your luggage, over-sized parcels, sport equipment (skis, golf clubs) etc. from any address to any other address in the country, including airports.

## YOU MAY WANT TO SAY...

| | | |
|---|---|---|
| Do you have small bottles of mineral water? | 小さいボトルのミネラルウオーターはありますか? | *chiisai botoru no mineraru uohtah wa arimas ka* |
| Have you got any... | …はありますか? | *...wa ari mas ka* |
| imported beer? | 輸入ビール | *yunyuu biiru* |
| stamps? | 切手 | *kitte* |
| tissues? | ティッシュ | *tisshu* |
| Can I send... | ここから … が送れますか? | *koko kara ... ga okure mas ka* |
| a fax? | ファックス | *fakkusu* |
| luggage? | 荷物 | *nimotsu* |
| I'll have this ..., please. | この … を下さい。 | *kono ... o kudasai* |
| Yes, please warm it up. | はい，温めてください。 | *hai, atatamete kudasai* |
| No, that's fine. | いいえ，結構です。 | *iie, kekkoh des* |

## at the convenience store

- I would like to send...

  …を送りたいんで すが

  ...o okuri tain des ga

    ski equipment

    スキー用品

    skii yohhin

- It contains fragile goods.

  壊れやすいものが入 っています。

  koware yasui mono ga haitte imas

- When will it be delivered?

  いつ着きますか？

  itsu tsuki mas ka?

### YOU MAY HEAR...

- お弁当を温めます か。

  obentoh o atatame mas ka?

  Would you like this box lunch warmed?

- はい，こちらです／ こちらにございま す。

  hai, kochira des/ kochira ni gozai mas

  Yes, over here.

- この用紙に記入し て下さい。

  kono yohshi ni kinyuu shite kudasai

  Please fill in this form.

- どちらに送ります か。

  dochira ni okuri mas ka?

  Where is it going?

- はい，送れます。

  hai, okure mas

  Yes, we can deliver it/them.

- 何が入っています か。

  nani ga haitte imas ka?

  What's in it?

- 明日／あさって着き ます。

  asu/asatte tsuki mas

  It'll be delivered tomorrow/the day after tomorrow.

# ✳ at the post office

● Post offices and post boxes have the symbol 〒, which is also placed before the postal code when writing a Japanese address. Stamps are also sold at convenience stores and station kiosks.

● Stamps can be purchased only after the size (cards) and weight (letters) are measured, apart from standardised cards and standard weight envelopes.

## YOU MAY WANT TO SAY...

| | | |
|---|---|---|
| I would like to post this, please. | これをお願いします。 | kore o onegai shimas |
| For ..., please.<br>America<br>UK | …です<br>アメリカ<br>イギリス | ...des<br>amerika<br>igirisu |
| Can I send this...<br><br>registered?<br>by air mail?<br><br>by seamail? | …で送りたいんで<br>すが?<br>書留<br>航空便/エアメール<br><br>船便 | ...de okurita in des ga<br><br>kakitome<br>kohkuu bin/ea<br>meiru<br>funa bin |
| It contains ...<br>a present<br>something<br>fragile | …が入っています<br>プレゼント<br>壊れやすい物 | ...ga haitte imas<br>purezento<br>koware yasui mono |
| Can I have a receipt, please? | レシートをお願いします。 | reshiito o onegai shimas |
| Do you change currency here? | ここで通貨の両替は出来ますか? | kokode tsuuka no ryohgae wa deki mas ka |

shops and services

159

## at the bank

| | | |
|---|---|---|
| どちらに送ります か？ | *dochira ni okuri mas ka* | **Where is it going?** |
| 何が入っています か？ | *nani ga haitte imas ka* | **What's in it?** |
| この税関告知書に 記入して下さい。 | *kono zeikan kokuchisho ni kinyuu shite kudasai* | **Please fill in this customs declaration form.** |

## ✳ at the bank

● Most Japanese banks are open from 9am to 3pm but only open their foreign exchange departments from 11am. The cash machines of Japanese banks usually only accept cards issued in Japan, and close at 6pm and at weekends.

● Cash machines which will accept foreign cards can be found at post offices, department stores and *konbini*.

### YOU MAY WANT TO SAY...

| | | |
|---|---|---|
| **Excuse me, where's the foreign exchange counter?** | すみませんが，外貨 両替所はどこですか？ | *sumimasen ga, gaika ryohgae jo wa doko des ka* |
| **Is there a cash point here?** | ここにＡＴＭはあり ますか？ | *koko ni ATM wa ari mas ka* |
| **The cash point machine has retained my card.** | カードがＡＴＭから 出てきません。 | *kahdo ga ATM kara dete kimasen* |

- **I've forgotten my pin number.**
  暗証番号を忘れてしまいました。
  *anshoh bangoh o wasurete shimai mashita*

- **I'd like to... withdraw some money**
  …たいんですが 現金を引き出し
  *...tain des ga genkin o hiki dashi*

### YOU MAY HEAR...

- パスポートはお持ちですか?
  *pasupohto wa omochi des ka*
  **Your passport, please.**

- お客様のお名前をお願いします。
  *okyaku sama no onamae o onegai shimas*
  **What's your name?**

- 手数料がかかりますが，よろしいですか?
  *tesuu ryoh ga kakari mas ga yoroshii des ka*
  **There's a charge. Would you like to continue?**

## ✳ changing money
(see **numbers** page 14)

- Japan's currency is the Yen (日本円), (*en*). The currency symbol can appear as either (¥) or (円). Yen coins come in denominations of 1, 5, 10, 50, 100 and 500. Bank notes come in denominations of 1,000, 2,000, 5,000 and 10,000.

### YOU MAY WANT TO SAY...

| | | |
|---|---|---|
| I'd like to change ... into Yen, please. | …を日本円にしたいんですが | ...o nihon en ni shitain des ga |
| these travellers' cheques | このトラベラーズチェック | kono toraberahzu chekku |
| one hundred pounds | 百ポンド | hyaku pondo |
| Can I have... | …お願いします。 | ...onegai shimas |
| some change? | 小銭を | kozeni o |
| ten ¥1,000 notes? | 千円札を十枚 | sen en satsu o juu mai |
| I'd like to take some money out on my credit card. | クレジットカードで現金を引き出したいんですが。 | kurejitto kahdo de genkin o hiki dashi tain des ga |
| What's the rate today... | 今日の … のレートはいくらですか? | kyoh no ... no reito wa ikura des ka |
| for the pound? | ポンド | pondo |
| for the US dollar? | 米ドル | bei doru |
| for the euro? | ユーロ | yuuro |

### YOU MAY HEAR...

| | | |
|---|---|---|
| おいくらですか? | oikura des ka | How much? |
| こちらにご署名をお願いします。 | kochira ni gosho mei o onegai shimas | Sign here, please. |
| 今日のレートは一ポンド二百三十円です。 | kyoh no reito wa ichi pondo nihyaku san juu en des | Today's rate is ¥230 to the Pound. |

# ✳ telephones

Public phones are not commonly used in Japan, as most people have mobile phones. They are mainly located at stations and airports. Pre-paid phone cards are widely available, at *konbini*, in station kiosks and from vending machines. An English-language directory is published for Tokyo and directory assistance (dial 104) is also available in English.

## YOU MAY WANT TO SAY...

| | | |
|---|---|---|
| I'd like to...<br>    buy a phone card<br>    call the UK<br><br>    make a reverse charge call | …たいんですが<br>テレホンカードを買い<br>イギリスに電話をかけ<br><br>コレクトコールをかけ | …*tain des ga*<br>    *terehon kahdo o kai*<br>    *igirisu ni denwa o kake*<br>    *korekuto kohru o kake* |
| The number is... | 電話番号は … です。 | *denwa bangoh wa … des* |
| How much does it cost, per minute? | 一分間いくらですか? | *ippun kan ikura des ka* |
| What's the country code? | 国番号は何番ですか? | *kuni ban goh wa nanban des ka* |
| How do I get an outside line? | どうやって外線にするんですか? | *doh yatte gaisen ni suru n des ka* |
| Hello. | もしもし。 | *moshi moshi* |
| May I have extension..., please? | 内線番号…をお願いします? | *naisen ban goh … o onegai shimas* |

| | | |
|---|---|---|
| May I speak to...? | …さんをお願いします。 | ...san o onegai shimas |
| I'll ring back. | あとで かけ直します。 | atode kake naoshi mas |
| May I leave a message? | 伝言をお願いできますか? | dengon o onegai dekimas ka |
| Could you say ... called? | …から電話があったと伝えてもらえますか? | ...kara denwa ga atta to tsutaete morae mas ka |

## YOU MAY HEAR...

| | | |
|---|---|---|
| もしもし, 田中です。 | moshi moshi, Tanaka des | Hello, this is the Tanaka residence. |
| 私です。 | watashi des | Speaking. |
| どなた様ですか? | donata sama des ka | Who's calling? |
| すみません。今, 留守にしています。 | sumimasen, ima rusu ni shite imas | Sorry, he/she's not here. |
| 少々お待ち下さい。 | shoh shoh omachi kudasai | Just a moment. |
| 話し中です。 | hanashi chuu des | It's engaged. |
| どなたもお出になりません。 | donata mo ode ni nari masen | There's no answer. |
| お待ちになりますか? | omachi ni narimas ka | Do you want to hold? |
| すみません。番号を間違えました。 | sumimasen. bangoh o machigae mashita | Sorry, wrong number. |

# ✳ mobiles

- Have you got a charger for this phone?

  この携帯電話の充電器はありますか?

  *kono keitai denwa no juudenki wa arimas ka*

- Can I/we hire a mobile?

  携帯電話を借りたいんですが?

  *keitai denwa o kari tain des ga*

- What's the tariff?

  料金はいくらですか?

  *ryohkin wa ikura des ka*

- Are text messages included?

  メールは含まれていますか?

  *meiru wa fuku marete imas ka*

- How do you dial a local call?

  市内通話をかけるにはどうしたらいいですか?

  *shinai denwa o kakeru niwa doh shitara ii des ka*

- How do you send text messages?

  メールはどうやって送るんですか?

  *meiru wa doh yatte okuru n des ka*

# ✳ the internet

- Is there an internet café near here?

  この辺にインターネットカフェがありますか?

  *kono hen ni intah netto kafe ga ari mas ka*

- How much is it per minute?

  一分間いくらですか?

  *ippun kan ikura des ka*

- I can't log-on.

  ログイン出来ません。

  *roguin deki masen*

- It's not connecting.

  接続出来ません。

  *setsuzoku deki masen*

| | | |
|---|---|---|
| It's very slow. | とても遅いんですが。 | totemo osoin des ga |
| Could you... | …していただけますか? | ...shite itadake mas ka |
| print this? | これを印刷 | kore o insatsu |
| scan this? | これをスキャン | kore o sukyan |
| Can I... | …いいですか? | ...ii des ka |
| download this? | これをダウンロードしても | kore o daunrohdo shitemo |
| use my memory stick? | メモリースティックを使っても | memorii sutikku o tsukattemo |
| Do you have a CD-Rom? | シーディーアールがありますか? | shii dii ahru ga arimas ka |

## YOU MAY SEE...

| | | |
|---|---|---|
| ユーザー名 | yuuzah mei | username |
| パスワード | pasuwahdo | password |
| ここをクリック | koko o kurikku | click here |
| リンク | rinku | link |

## ✳ faxes

## YOU MAY WANT TO SAY...

| | | |
|---|---|---|
| What's your fax number? | ファックス番号を教えて下さい。 | fakkusu bangoh o oshiete kudasai |
| Could you send this fax, please? | これをファックスしていただけませんか? | kore o fakkusu shite itadake masen ka |
| How much is it? | いくらですか? | ikura des ka |

# health&safety

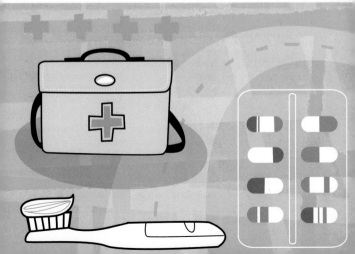

# ✳ at the chemist's

● Look for the sign 薬 (*kusuri* meaning 'medicine') when looking for a chemist or drugstore 薬局 (*yakkyoku*). *Yakkyoku* sell over-the-counter and prescription medicines, as well as toiletries, cosmetics, baby foods and health care products. Medicines manufactured in Japan may have different brand names, and are either lower-strength or prescribed in lower dosages than in Europe.

## YOU MAY SEE...

| | | |
|---|---|---|
| 毎食後 | *mai shokugo* | after every meal |
| 就寝前/寝る前 | *shuushin mae/neru mae* | before bedtime |
| カプセル | *kapuseru* | capsule |
| 外用専用/外用のみ | *gaiyoh senyoh/gaiyoh nomi* | for external use only |
| 1日3回7日分 | *ichi nichi san kai, nanoka bun* | for seven days, three times-a-day |
| 食後すぐに | *shokugo suguni* | immediately after a meal |
| 錠剤 | *joh zai* | tablet |
| 食事の30分後 | *shokuji no sanjuppun go* | thirty minutes after eating |
| 食事の30分前 | *shokuji no sanjuppun mae* | thirty minutes before eating |
| 散剤/こな薬 | *sanzai/kona gusuri* | powder |
| 処方箋 | *shohou sen* | prescription |

## YOU MAY WANT TO SAY...

| | | |
|---|---|---|
| Are you a pharmacist? | 薬剤師さんですか? | yakuzaishi san des ka |
| Have you got something for... | …に効く薬がありますか? | ...ni kiku kusuri ga arimas ka |
| sunburn? | 日焼け | hiyake |
| diarrhoea? | 下痢 | geri |
| period pains? | 生理痛 | seiritsuu |
| headaches? | 頭痛 | zu tsuu |
| stomach ache? | 胃痛 | itsuu |
| a sore throat? | のどの痛み | nodo no itami |
| I need some... please | …が欲しいんですが | ...ga hoshii n des ga |
| aspirin | 鎮痛剤/アスピリン | chintsuuzai/asupirin |
| condoms | コンドーム | kondohmu |
| disinfectant | 消毒薬 | shoudoku yaku |
| eye drops | 目薬 | megusuri |
| insect repellent | 虫除け | mushiyoke |
| painkillers | 痛み止め | itami dome |
| plasters | 絆創膏 | bansohkoh |
| sanitary towels | ナプキン | napkin |
| suntan lotion | 日焼け用のローション | hiyakeyoh no roushon |
| tampons | タンポン | tanpon |
| toilet paper | トイレットペーパー | toiretto peipah |
| toothpaste | 歯磨き粉 | hamigaki ko |
| travel sickness pills | 乗り物酔いの薬 | norimono yoi no kusuri |

## YOU MAY HEAR...

| 今までにこの薬を飲んだことがありますか？ | ima made ni kono kusuri o non da koto ga arimas ka | Have you taken this before? |
| 処方箋はお持ちですか | shohoh sen wa omochi des ka | Have you got a prescription? |
| これを一日三回飲んで下さい。 | kore o ichinichi san kai nonde kudasai | Take this three times a day. |
| この錠剤を一日二回一錠ずつ飲んで下さい。 | kono jouzai o ichi nichi nikai ichijou zutsu nonde kudasai | Take one tablet twice a day. |
| 食前／食後に飲んで下さい。 | shoku zen/shoku go ni non de kudasai | To be taken before/after meals. |

## ✳ at the doctor's
(see **medical complaints and conditions**, page 174)

● Doctors in Japan do not make house-calls, or see patients at weekends or in the evenings.

● A list of English-speaking doctors is available from the British Embassy in Tokyo, and from the International Association for Medical Assistance to Travellers *www.iamat. org*. It is advisable to know your blood type and to have this noted on any travel insurance or medical documents you bring with you.

## YOU MAY SEE...

| | | |
|---|---|---|
| 診療申込書 | *shinryoh moushi komi sho* | application for examination and treatment |
| 会計/精算 | *kaikei/seisan* | cashier |
| 精算受付 | *seisan uketsuke* | cashier reception |
| 受診 | *jushin* | consultation |
| 新患受付 | *shinkan uketsuke* | reception for new patients |
| 再診受付 | *saishin uketsuke* | reception for registered patients |

## YOU MAY WANT TO SAY...

- **I need a doctor (who speaks English).**
  英語ができる医者を探しています。
  *eigo ga dekiru isha o sagashite imas*

- **Can I make an appointment for...**
  …予約はできますか?
  *...yoyaku wa deki mas ka*

  | today? | 今日の | *kyoh no* |
  | tomorrow? | 明日の | *asu/ashita no* |
  | next Monday? | 来週の月曜日の | *raishuu no getsu yohbi no* |

- **I've run out of my medication.**
  いつも飲んでいる薬がなくなってしまいました。
  *itsumo nondeiru kusuri ga naku natte shimai mashita*

- **I'm on medication for...**
  …の薬をのんでいます。
  *...no kusuri o non de imas*

| | | |
|---|---|---|
| I've had a... jab | …の予防注射をしました | ...no yoboh chuusha o shimashita |
| tetanus | 破傷風 | hashoufuu |
| typhoid | 腸チフス | choo chifuss |
| rabies | 狂犬病 | kyoukenbyoh |
| My daughter/son has had a ... vaccination for... | 娘/息子は… のワクチンを接種しました。 | musume/musuko wa... no wakuchin o sesshu shimashita |
| polio | ポリオ | porio |
| measles | はしか | hashika |
| Can I have a receipt for my health insurance, please? | 保険申請用のレシートをお願いします。 | hoken shinsei yoh no reshiito o onegai shimas |

## ✳ describing your symptoms
(see **parts of the body**, see page 178)

Doctors (and dentists) are addressed as *sensei* (先生), nurses are addressed as *kangoshi san* (看護師さん). Be aware that Japanese doctors are not used to being asked to explain themselves to patients.

### YOU MAY WANT TO SAY...

| | | |
|---|---|---|
| I don't feel well. | 気分が良くないです。 | kibun ga yokunai des |
| I need to lie down. | 横になりたいです。 | yoko ni naritai des |
| It hurts here. | ここが痛みます。 | koko ga itami mas |

- My... hurts …が痛いです ...ga itai des
  - feet 足 ashi
  - head 頭 atama
  - stomach 胃 i

- I've got...
  - a sore throat 喉が痛いです。 nodo ga itai des
  - diarrhoea 下痢をしています geri o shite imas
  - a bad 頭がとても痛い atama ga totemo
    headache です itai des

- I'm dizzy. めまいがします。 memai ga shimas

- I feel... …です ...des
  - feverish 熱っぽい netsuppoi
  - sluggish 体がだるい karada ga darui
  - sick 吐きそう hakisou

- I can't... …が出来ません ...ga deki masen
  - breathe うまく呼吸 umaku kokyuu
    properly
  - sleep properly 夜眠ること yoru nemuru koto

- My nose is 鼻血が出ています。 hanaji ga dete imas
  bleeding.

- I'm bleeding. 出血しています。 shukketsu shite imas

- I've cut/burnt けが/火傷をしまいま kega/yakedo o
  myself. した。 shimashita

- I've been sick. 吐きました。 haki mashita

- I feel a little 少し良くなりまし sukoshi yoku nari
  better. た。 mashita

## ✳ medical complaints and conditions

| | | |
|---|---|---|
| I'm...<br>arthritic<br>asthmatic | …があります<br>関節炎<br>ぜん息 | ...ga arimas<br>kansetsu en<br>zensoku |
| I'm blind. | 目が見えません。 | me ga mie masen |
| I'm deaf. | 耳が聞こえません。 | mimi ga kikoe masen |
| I'm...<br>diabetic<br>epileptic | …です。<br>糖尿病<br>てんかん | ...des<br>toh nyoh byoh<br>tenkan |
| I'm pregnant. | 妊娠しています。 | ninshin shite imas |
| I've got...<br>high/low blood<br>pressure | …です<br>高血圧<br>低血圧 | ...des<br>koh ketsuatsu<br>tei ketsuatsu |
| My blood type is O. | 血液型は0型です。 | ketsueki gata wa oh gata des |
| I have a pain in my chest. | 胸が苦しいです。 | mune ga kurushii des |
| I've got a heart condition. | 心臓が悪いんです。 | shinzoh ga waru in des |
| I use a wheelchair. | 車椅子を使っています。 | kuruma isu o tsukatte imas |
| I have difficulty walking. | 歩行が困難です。 | hokoh ga konnan des |
| I'm HIV positive. | エイズウイルスに感染しています。 | eizu uirusu ni kansen shite imas |

- I'm allergic to... …のアレルギーがあ ...no arerugii ga
  ります arimas

  antibiotics 抗生物質 kohsei busshitsu
  cortisone コーチゾン kohchizon
  nuts ナッツ類 nattsurui
  penicillin ペニシリン penishirin

- I suffer from... …があります。 ...ga arimas
  hay fever 花粉症 kafun shoh

## YOU MAY HEAR...

| | | |
|---|---|---|
| ここで少々お待ち下さい。 | kokode shoh shoh omachi kudasai | Please wait here a moment. |
| どこが痛いですか? | doko ga itai des ka | Where does it hurt? |
| ここは痛いですか? | koko wa itai des ka | Does it hurt here? |
| いつから、この症状がありますか? | itsukara kono shohjoh ga arimas ka | How long have you been feeling like this? |
| 何か薬を飲んでいますか? | nani ka kusuri o nonde imas ka? | Are you on medication? |
| 高血圧だったことはありますか? | kohketsuatsu datta koto wa arimas ka | Have you got a history of high blood pressure? |
| アレルギーがありますか? | arerugiii ga arimas ka | Are you allergic to anything? |
| おいくつですか? | oikutsu des ka | How old are you? |
| 口を開けて下さい。 | kuchi o akete kudasai | Open your mouth, please. |

health and safety

175

# medical complaints and conditions

| | | |
|---|---|---|
| …を計ります | …o hakari mas | I need to take your… |
| 血圧 | ketsuatsu | blood pressure |
| 脈 | myaku | pulse |
| 体温 | taion | temperature |
| 服を脱いで下さい。 | fuku o nuide kudasai | Get undressed, please. |
| ここに横になって下さい。 | koko ni yoko ni natte kudasai | Lie down here, please. |
| …に寝て下さい | …ni nete kudasai | Lie…, please. |
| 仰向け | aomuke | on your back |
| 横向き | yoko muki | on your side |
| うつぶせ | utsubuse | on your stomach |
| 深刻な病気じゃありません。 | shinkoku na byohki ja arimasen | It's nothing serious. |
| 感染症にかかっています。 | kansenshoh ni kakatte imas | You've got an infection. |
| …の検査をします。 | …no kensa o shimas | I need a… sample. |
| 血液 | ketsueki | blood |
| 尿 | nyoh | urine |
| 便 | ben | stool |
| レントゲンを撮ります。 | rentogen o tori mas | You need an X-ray. |
| 注射をします。 | chuusha o shimas | I'm going to give you an injection. |
| ペニシリンのアレルギーがありますか? | penishirin no arerugii ga arimas ka | Are you allergic to penicillin? |
| 安静にして下さい。 | ansei ni shite kudasai | You must rest. |

| …で下さい。 | …de kudasai | You mustn't… |
| お酒を飲まない | osake o nomanai | drink alcohol |
| 今晩お風呂に入らない | konban ofuro ni hairanai | take a bath tonight |
| 帰国後、医師の診察を受けて下さい。 | kikoku go ishi no shinsatsu o ukete kudasai | You should see a doctor when you go home. |
| 病院へ行って下さい。 | byohin e itte kudasai | You need to go to hospital. |
| …を捻挫しています | …o nenza shite imas | You've sprained your… |
| 足首 | ashikubi | ankle |
| 手首 | tekubi | wrist |
| …が折れています。 | …ga orete imas | You've broken your… |
| 腕 | ude | arm |
| 肋骨 | rokkotsu | ribs |
| …です。 | …des | You've got… |
| インフルエンザ | infuruenza | flu |
| 虫垂炎/盲腸炎 | chuusui en/moh choh en | appendicitis |
| 気管支炎 | kikanshi en | bronchitis |
| 食中毒です。 | shoku chuu doku des | You've got food poisoning. |
| 骨折しています。 | kossetsu shite imas | You've got a fracture. |
| 心臓発作です。 | shinzoh hossa des | It's a heart attack. |
| また三日後に来て下さい。 | mata mikka go ni kite kudasai | You must come back in three days' time. |

health and safety

177

## ✳ parts of the body

● There is no distinction in Japanese between singular and plural. *Ude* (腕), for example, means both 'arm' and 'arms'.

### YOU MAY WANT TO SAY...

| | | |
|---|---|---|
| ankle | あしくび | *ashikubi* |
| appendix | ちゅうすい/もうちょう | *chuusui/mohchoh* |
| arm | うで | *ude* |
| armpit | わきのした | *wakinoshita* |
| artery | どうみゃく | *dohmyaku* |
| back | せなか | *senaka* |
| bladder | ぼうこう | *bohkoh* |
| blood | ち/けつえき | *chi/ketsueki* |
| blood vessel | けっかん | *kekkan* |
| body | からだ | *karada* |
| bone | ほね | *hone* |
| bottom | おしり | *oshiri* |
| bowels | ちょう | *choh* |
| breast | むね | *mune* |
| calf | ふくらはぎ | *fukurahagi* |
| cheek | ほお | *hoh* |
| chest | むね | *mune* |
| chin | あご | *ago* |
| collar bone | さこつ | *sakotsu* |
| ear | みみ | *mimi* |
| earlobe | みみたぶ | *mimitabu* |
| elbow | ひじ | *hiji* |
| eye | め | *me* |
| eyebrow | まゆ | *mayu* |

health and safety

178

| | | |
|---|---|---|
| eyelid | まぶた | *mabuta* |
| face | かお | *kao* |
| finger | ゆび | *yubi* |
| foot | あし | *ashi* |
| forehead | ひたい | *hitai* |
| genitals | せいしょくき | *seishokuki* |
| gland (lymph) | リンパせん | *rinpasen* |
| gum | はぐき | *haguki* |
| hair | かみ/け | *kami/ke* |
| hand | て | *te* |
| head | あたま | *atama* |
| heart | しんぞう | *shinzoh* |
| heel | かかと | *kakato* |
| hip | おしり | *oshiri* |
| jaw | あご | *ago* |
| joint | かんせつ | *kansetsu* |
| kidney | じんぞう | *jinzoh* |
| knee | ひざ | *hiza* |
| leg | あし | *ashi* |
| ligament | じんたい | *jintai* |
| lip | くちびる | *kuchibiru* |
| liver | かんぞう | *kanzoh* |
| lung | はい | *hai* |
| mouth | くち | *kuchi* |
| muscle | きんにく | *kinniku* |
| nail | つめ | *tsume* |
| neck | くび | *kubi* |
| nerve | しんけい | *shinkei* |
| nose | はな | *hana* |
| palm | てのひら | *tenohira* |
| penis | ペニス | *penisu* |

health and safety

179

| | | |
|---|---|---|
| rib | ろっこつ | *rokkotsu* |
| shin | すね | *sune* |
| shoulder | かた | *kata* |
| skin | はだ | *hada* |
| sole | あしのうら | *ashinoura* |
| spine | せきつい | *sekitsui* |
| stomach | い | *i* |
| temple | こめかみ | *komekami* |
| tendon | けん | *ken* |
| testicle | こうがん | *kohgan* |
| thigh | もも | *momo* |
| throat | のど | *nodo* |
| thumb | おやゆび | *oyayubi* |
| toe | つまさき | *tsumasaki* |
| tongue | した | *shita* |
| tonsils | へんとうせん | *hentohsen* |
| tooth | は | *ha* |
| vagina | ちつ | *chitsu* |
| vein | じょうみゃく | *johmyaku* |
| waist | こし/ウエスト | *koshi/uesuto* |
| wrist | てくび | *tekubi* |

## ✳ at the dentist's

● Dental surgeries are usually closed on Thursdays and Sundays. Unlike doctors, dentists in Japan operate an appointment system.

## YOU MAY WANT TO SAY...

| | | |
|---|---|---|
| I need a dentist (who speaks English). | 英語ができる歯医者を探しています。 | eigo ga dekiru haisha o sagashite imas |
| I've got toothache. | 歯が痛いです。 | ha ga itai des |
| It (really) hurts. | （とても）痛いです。 | (totemo) itai des |
| It's my wisdom tooth. | 親知らずです。 | oya shirazu des |
| I've lost ... | …がとれてしまいました | ...ga torete shimai mashita |
| a filling | 詰め物 | tsume mono |
| a crown/cap | かぶせ物 | kabuse mono |
| I've broken a tooth. | 歯が欠けてしまいました。 | ha ga kakete shimai mashita |
| Can you fix it temporarily? | 応急処置ができますか。 | ohkyu shochi ga dekimas ka |
| How long will it take? | どのくらいかかりますか？ | dono kurai kakari mas ka |

## YOU MAY HEAR...

| | | |
|---|---|---|
| 大きく開けて。 | ohkiku akete | Open wide. |
| 口を閉じて。 | kuchi o tojite | Close your jaws together. |
| レントゲンを撮ります。 | rentogen o tori mas | You need an x-ray. |
| 妊娠していますか？ | ninshin shite imas ka | Are you pregnant? |

| 詰め物がいります。 | tsume mono ga irimas | You need a filling. |
| 抜かなければなりません。 | nukanakereba nari masen | I'll have to take it out. |
| …をします | ...o shimas | I'm going to give you… |
| 注射 | chuusha | an injection |
| 一時的な詰め物 | ichiji teki na tsume mono | a temporary filling |
| 一時的なかぶせ物 | ichi ji teki na kabuse mono | a temporary crown |
| 健康保健証がありますか? | kenkoh hoken shoh ga arimas ka | Do you have a Japanese National Health Insurance card? |
| 申し訳ありませんが、実費になります。 | mohshi wake arimasen ga jippi ni nari mas | Sorry, but you must pay the full cost. |

## \* emergencies

● Emergency ambulance services are free, but you will be asked for details of your health insurance. Call the numbers below for the following services:

| EMERGENCIES | |
| --- | --- |
| Police: **110** | Ambulance: **119** |
| Fire: **119** | Marine Emergencies: **118** |

## YOU MAY SEE...

| | | |
|---|---|---|
| 救急病院 | kyuu kyuu byohin | Accident and Emergency |
| 救急車 | kyuu kyuu sha | ambulance |
| 医院/クリニック | i in/kurinikku | clinic (normally a small private surgery) |
| 歯科医院/クリニック | shika i in/shika kurinikku | dental surgery/clinic |
| 歯医者 | haisha | dentist |
| 医師 | ishi | doctor |
| 緊急医療サービス | kin kyuu iryoh sahbisu | emergency services |
| 消火器 | shohkaki | fire extinguisher |
| 応急処置 | ohkyuu shochi | first aid |
| 病院 | byohin | hospital |
| 使用方法 | shiyoh houhou | instructions for use |
| 看護師 | kangoshi | nurse |
| 手術 | shujutsu | operation |
| 毒 | doku | poison |
| 交番 | kohban | police box (sub-station) |
| 警察署 | keisatsu sho | police station |
| 診療時間 | shinryoh jikan | surgery times |

## YOU MAY WANT TO SAY...

- I need...   …を呼んで下さい   ...o yonde kudasai
  - a doctor   医者   isha
  - an ambulance   救急車   kyuu kyuu sha
  - the fire brigade   消防車   shoh boh sha
  - the police   警察   keisatsu

| | | |
|---|---|---|
| Immediately! | すぐにお願いします。 | *suguni onegai shimas* |
| It's very urgent! | 緊急です。 | *kinkyuu des* |
| Help! | 助けて。 | *tasukete* |
| Please help me/us. | 助けて下さい。 | *tasu kete kudasai* |
| Please take me/us to the hospital. | 病院に連れて行って下さい。 | *byohin ni tsurete itte kudasai* |
| There's a fire! | 火事です。 | *kaji des* |
| There's been an accident. | 事故がありました。 | *jiko ga arimashita* |
| I have to use the phone. | 電話をかけたいです。 | *denwa o kake tai des* |
| I'm lost. | 今いる場所がどこか、わかりません。 | *ima iru basho ga dokoka wakarimasen* |
| I've lost my car keys. | 車の鍵をなくしてしまいました。 | *kuruma no kagi o nakushite shimai mashita.* |
| I've lost my daughter/son. | 娘/息子がいなくなってしまいました。 | *musume/musuko ga inaku natte shimai mashita* |
| I've left my... in a taxi.<br>    bag | タクシーに…を置き忘れました<br>    かばん | *takushii ni...o okiwasure mashita<br>    kaban* |
| Stop! | 止まれ。 | *tomare* |

## YOU MAY HEAR...

| | | |
|---|---|---|
| 119番です。 | hyaku juukyuu ban des | This is 119. |
| 何があったのか説明して下さい。 | nani ga attanoka setsumei shite kudasai | Please explain what happened. |
| お名前は？ | onamae wa | What is your name? |
| 住所はどちらですか。 | juusho wa dochira des ka | What's your address? |
| 今どこにいますか。 | ima doko ni imas ka | Where are you now? |

## YOU MAY WANT TO SAY...

| | | |
|---|---|---|
| There's a fire. | 火事です。 | kaji des |
| It is at... (place) | 場所は … です。 | basho wa ... des |
| We need an ambulance. | 救急車をお願いします。 | kyuu kyuu sha o onegai shimas |
| The address is... | 住所は … です。 | juusho wa ... des |
| There's been an accident. | 事故です。 | jiko des |
| Someone is ill. | 急病人が出ました。 | kyuu byoh nin ga demashita |
| It's near the station. | 駅の近くです。 | eki no chikaku des |

health and safety

185

## YOU MAY HEAR...

| | | |
|---|---|---|
| 事故ですか、急病ですか。 | jiko des ka, kyuu byoh des ka | Is it an accident or a sudden illness? |
| どうしましたか。 | doh shimashita ka | What happened? |
| 何か目印になるものが近くにありますか。 | nanika mejirushi ni naru mono ga chikaku ni arimas ka | Are there any landmarks nearby? |
| 名前をお願いします。 | namae o onegai shimas | Your name, please. |

## ✳ earthquakes

Reports on the severity of earthquakes 地震 (jishin) in Japan use the Shindo scale (1–7), as well as the Richter Scale. Shindo measures an earthquake's intensity at specific locations (rather than at its epi-centre). Readings above 4 mean a severe quake and damage.

## YOU MAY SEE...

| | | |
|---|---|---|
| 非難場所 | hinan basho | assembly (evacuation) point |
| 災害 | saigai | disaster |
| 緊急事態 | kinkyuu jitai | emergency |
| 地震速報 | jishin sokuhoh | earthquake news flash |

# * police

● Japanese police are armed. In urban areas *kohban* (交番) or police 'boxes' are commonplace. They are located near stations, shopping and residential areas, and are useful if you need local information or are lost.

## YOU MAY WANT TO SAY...

| | | |
|---|---|---|
| ● Sorry, I didn't realise it was against the law. | すみません。法律違反だと気づきませんでした。 | *Sumimasen. Hohritsu ihan dato kizuki masen deshita* |
| ● I haven't got my passport on me. | 今、手元にパスポートがありません。 | *ima, temoto ni pasupohto ga ari masen* |
| ● I don't understand. | わかりません。 | *wakarimasen* |
| ● I'm innocent. | 私は無実です。 | *watashi wa mujitsu des* |
| ● I need an English-speaking lawyer. | 英語がわかる弁護士を呼んで下さい。 | *eigo ga wakaru bengoshi o yonde kudasai* |
| ● I want to contact my... | …に連絡したいです | *...ni renraku shitai des* |
| embassy | 大使館 | *taishikan* |
| consulate | 領事館 | *ryohjikan* |

### YOU MAY HEAR...

| | | |
|---|---|---|
| 110番です。 | *hyaku toh ban des* | This is 110. |
| 罰金を払うことになります。 | *bakkin o harau koto ni nari mas* | You'll have to pay a fine. |
| 身分証明書をお持ちですか。 | *mibun syoumeisho o omochi des ka* | Have you got any proof of your identity? |
| 私と一緒に来て下さい。 | *watashi to isshoni kite kudasai* | Come with me. |
| 逮捕します。 | *taiho shimas* | You're under arrest. |

## ✳ reporting crime

● Telephone 110 or visit the nearest *kohban* to find out where the closest police station (警察署) is. In Tokyo, there is a dedicated police help-line, with English-speaking staff.

### YOU MAY WANT TO SAY...

| | | |
|---|---|---|
| I want to report a theft. | 盗難にあいました。 | *tohnan ni aimashita* |
| My ... has been stolen | … を盗まれました | *... o nusumare mashita* |
|    handbag | ハンドバッグ | *hando baggu* |
|    laptop | ノートパソコン | *nohto pasokon* |
|    purse/wallet | 財布 | *saifu* |
|    passport | パスポート | *pasupohto* |
| Our car has been broken into. | 車の中のものを盗まれました。 | *kuruma no naka no mono o nusumare mashita* |

- **Our car has been stolen.** 車を盗まれました。 *kuruma o nusumare mashita*

- **I've lost my...** … をなくしました *...o nakushi mashita*
  credit cards クレジットカード *kurejitto kahdo*
  luggage 荷物 *nimotsu*

- **I've been mugged.** 強盗にあいました。 *gohtoh ni aimashita*

- **I've been attacked.** 襲われました。 *osoware mashita*

## YOU MAY HEAR...

- いつ起こりました か？ *itsu okori mashita ka* **When did it happen?**

- どこでですか？ *doko de des ka* **Where?**

- 何があったんです か？ *nani ga attan des ka* **What happened?**

- その人は、どんな 人でしたか？ *sono hito wa, donna hito deshita ka* **What did he/she look like?**

- その人たちは、ど んな人たちでした か？ *sono hito tachi wa, donna hito tachi deshita ka* **What did they look like?**

## YOU MAY WANT TO SAY...

- It happened...
  five minutes ago
  last night
  on the beach

  …起こりました
  五分前に

  きのうの晩
  海岸で

  *okori mashita*
  *gofun mae ni*

  *kinoh no ban*
  *kaigan de*

- He/She had a knife.

  その人は、ナイフを
  持っていました。

  *sono hito wa naifu o motte imashita*

- He/She was...

  tall
  young
  short

  その人は… でした

  背が高い人
  若い人
  背が低い人

  *sono hito wa... deshita*
  *se ga takai hito*
  *wakai hito*
  *se ga hikui hito*

- The man was wearing a black T-shirt.

  その男の人は、黒い
  Tシャツを着ていま
  した。

  *sono otoko no hito wa, kuroi tiishatsu o kite imashita*

- The woman was wearing jeans.

  その女の人は、ジー
  ンズをはいていまし
  た。

  *sono onna no hito wa, jiinzu o haite imashita*

# basic grammar

## ✳ nouns

Japanese nouns do not have different genders, and there are no plural forms.

## ✳ articles

There are no definite or indefinite articles in Japanese. Instead, Japanese uses 'this/that', based on the proximity of the object to the speaker or listener.

Kore is used with things which are close to the speaker and translates as 'this'.

Sore (that) is used with things closer to the listener.

Are (that one over there) is used when the object referred to isn't close to either speaker or listener

| ARTICLES | | | |
|---|---|---|---|
| dore? which? | kore/korera this/these | sore/sorera that/those | are/arera that/those over there |
| doko? where? | koko here | soko there | asoko over there |

## ✳ adjectives

As in English, adjectives come before the noun they describe. There are two groups of adjectives: '-i' adjective and '-na' adjectives. In Japanese, adjectives change endings when you use them in the negative form or the past tense.

## ● '-i' adjectives

Most Japanese adjectives come into this group. They end in '-ai', '-oi', '-ii' or '-ui'.

| | |
|---|---|
| chiisai | small |
| omoshiroi | interesting |
| tanoshii | enjoyable |
| warui | bad |

| TENSE | ENDING | EXAMPLE |
|---|---|---|
| PRESENT AND SIMPLE FUTURE | -i des | omoshiroi des<br>it's interesting |
| PRESENT AND SIMPLE FUTURE NEGATIVE | -kunai des | omoshirokunai des<br>it isn't interesting |
| PAST | -katta des | omoshirokatta des<br>it was interesting |
| PAST NEGATIVE | -kunakatta des | omoshirokunakatta des<br>it wasn't interesting |

ii (good) is the only irregular adjective.

ii des   it's good

yokunai des   it isn't good

yokatta des   it was good

yokunakatta des   it wasn't good

## ● '-na' adjectives

shinsetsu, shinsetsu na   kind

Tanaka san wa shinsetsu des.   Mr/Ms Tanaka is kind.

Tanaka san wa shinsetsu na hito des.   Mr/Ms Tanaka is a kind person.

| TENSE | ENDING | EXAMPLE |
|---|---|---|
| **PRESENT AND SIMPLE FUTURE** | | benri des<br>it's convenient |
| **PRESENTAND SIMPLE FUTURE NEGATIVE** | - ja arimasen | benri ja arimasen<br>it isn't convenient |
| **PAST** | - deshita | benri deshita<br>it was convenient |
| **PAST NEGATIVE** | - ja arimasen deshita | benri ja arimasen deshita<br>it wasn't convenient |

## ✳ subject pronouns

When two people are talking, 'you' is not usually used.
Instead, refer to the other person by using their surname plus
san, e.g. Tanaka san.

## ✳ verbs

In Japanese, the patterns of verbs are the same in both the
singular and plural. The '-mas' ending form is polite, and is
used in this book.

| TENSE | AFFIRMATIVE FORM | NEGATIVE FORM |
|---|---|---|
| **PRESENT AND SIMPLE FUTURE TENSE** | tabe mas<br>eat/will eat | tabe masen<br>don't eat/won't eat |
| **PAST TENSE** | tabe mashita<br>ate | tabe masendeshita<br>didn't eat |

The forms of verbs are not affected by the topic or the subject.

Sushi o tabe mas.  I eat/will eat Sushi.

Tanaka san wa Sushi o tabe mas.  Ms Tanaka eats/will eat Sushi.

Kare/kanojo wa Sushi o tabe mas   He/she eats/will eat
Sushi.

Watashitachi wa Sushi o tabe mas   We eat/will eat.

Karera wa Sushi o tabe mas   They eat/will eat.

## ✳ word order

The structure of a Japanese sentence is: subject – object
– verb, rather than subject – verb – object as in English.

## ✳ questions

This is done simply by adding -*ka* to the end of a verb, the
verb remains unchanged.

Tanaka san wa Sushi o tabemas ka.   Does Mr/Ms Tanaka
eat Sushi?

| QUESTION WORD | |
|---|---|
| dare<br>Ano hito wa dare des ka? | who<br>Who is that person? |
| itsu<br>Tanjyohbi wa itsu des ka? | when<br>When is your birthday? |
| doko<br>Eki wa doko des ka? | where<br>Where is the station? |
| ikura<br>Ikura des ka? | how much<br>How much is it? |
| donokurai<br>Tokyo kara Kyoto made<br>donokurai kakari mas ka? | how long<br>How long does it take from<br>Tokyo to Kyoto? |

# ✳ particles

Japanese doesn't have prepositions, particles are used. They come after the word or phrase they refer to, and help define the role of subjects and objects. For example, 'wa' is a topic marker ,'ga' is a subject marker and 'o' is an object marker.

Tanaka san wa sushi o tabemas.   Mr/Ms Tanaka eats Sushi.

# ✳ counters

Objects are allocated counters according to their shape or nature. If in doubt use the generic counter, or cardinal numbers.

● **generic counters** (which come after the object) include:

| | |
|---|---|
| ...hitotsu | 1... |
| ...futatsu | 2... |
| ...mittsu | 3... |
| ...yottsu | 4... |
| ...itsutsu | 5... |
| ...muttsu | 6... |
| ...nanatsu | 7... |
| ...yattsu | 8... |
| ...kokonotsu | 9... |
| ...toh | 10... |

kohii o hitotsu onegai shimas   One coffee, please.

● **specific counters** counters include:

-ko for small objects, usually foods

| | |
|---|---|
| tamago ikko | 1 egg |
| meron niko | 2 melons |

-mai for flat objects, such as tickets, stamps, photos, even chocolate bars

| | |
|---|---|
| kitte ichimai | 1 (stamp) |
| kippu nimai | 2 (tickets) |
| shashin sanmai | 3 (photos) |

-hon/pon/bon for long, thin objects, e.g. bottles, cigarettes, pens. Whether the sound used is -hon or -pon or -bon depends on the sound which comes immediately before the counter

ippon...
nihon...
sanbon...

-nin is used for counting people (except one person and two people)

| | |
|---|---|
| hitori | one person |
| futari | two people |
| san nin | three people |
| yo nin | four people |
| go nin | five people |

# English – Japanese Dictionary

There is no distinction between singular-plural forms of nouns; the nouns listed may be used as either the singular or plural form (e.g. 日本人 *nihonjin* can mean either 'Japanese (person)' or 'Japanese (people)'.

Verbs are shown in the *-mas* (–ます) or polite form, and are suitable for all occasions.

There's a list of **car parts** on page 75 and **parts of the body** on page 178. See also the **menu reader** on page 116, and **numbers** on page 14.

## A

**abacus** そろばん *soroban*
**about** (*approximately*) およそ *oyoso*
&raquo; (*relating to*) -について *-ni tsuite*
**abroad** 外国で/に *gaikoku de/ni*
to **accept** 受け入れます/認めます *ukeiremas/mitomemas*
**accident** 事故 *jiko*
**accommodation** 宿泊施設 *shukuhaku shisetsu*
**ache** 痛み *itami*
**across** (*opposite*) –の向こう側に *-no mukoh gawa ni*
**actor** 俳優 *haiyuu*
**actress** 女優 *joyuu*
**adaptor** アダプター *adaputah*
**addict** 中毒者 *chuudoku sha*
**addicted** 中毒の/熱狂的な *chuudoku no/nekkyoh tekina*
**address** 住所 *juusho*
**admission charge** 入場料 *nyuujoh ryoh*
**adult** 大人 *otona*
**advance** (*payment*) 前金 *maekin*
&raquo; **in advance** あらかじめ *arakajime*

**advertisement, advertising** 広告/宣伝 *koukoku/senden*
**aeroplane** 飛行機 *hikohki*
**after** –の後で *-no ato de*
&raquo; **afterwards** その後 *sono go*
**afternoon** 午後 *gogo*
**again** もう一度 *mohichido*
**ago** 前に *maeni*
to **agree** 同意/賛成します *dohi/sansei shimas*
**air conditioning** エアコン *eakon*
**air mail** エアメール *ea meiru*
**airport** 空港 *kuukoh*
**aisle** 通路 *tsuuro*
**alarm** 警報 *keihoh*
&raquo; **alarm clock** めざまし時計 *mezamashi dokei*
**alcohol** アルコール *arukohru*
**all** 全部 *zenbu*
**allergic** アレルギーの *areruigii no*
**all right** (*OK*) 大丈夫 *daijohbu*
**already** もう *moh*
**also** 〜も *-mo*
**always** いつも *itsumo*
**America** アメリカ *amerika*

**anaesthetic** (*local*) 麻酔 (局部麻酔) *masui (kyokubu masui)*
» (*general*) (全身麻酔) *zenshin masui*
**and** と/そして *to/soshite*
**angry** 怒った *okotta*
**animal** 動物 *dohbutsu*
**anniversary** 記念日 *kinenbi*
**any** どれでも/いくらか *dore demo/ ikuraka*
**anyone** 誰でも/誰か *dare demo/ dareka*
**anything** 何でも/何か *nan demo/ nanika*
**anywhere** どこでも/どこかに *doko demo/dokokani*
**apartment block** マンション *manshon*
**appetite** 食欲 *shoku yoku*
to **apply** 申し込みます *mohshi komi mas*
**appointment** 約束/任命 *yaku soku/ ninmei*
**approximately** だいたい/約 *dai tai/yaku*
**archipelago** 諸島 *shotoh*
**architect** 建築家 *kenchiku ka*
**armbands** (*swimming*) 浮き輪 *ukiwa*
**army** 陸軍 *rikugun*
to **arrange** 準備/手配します *junbi/tehai shimas*
**arrival** 到着 *tohchaku*
to **arrive** 到着します *tohchaku shimas*
**art** 芸術/美術 *geijutsu/bijutsu*
**artificial** 不自然な/人工の *fushizen na/jinkoh no*
**artist** 芸術家/画家 *geijutsu ka/gaka*
**ashtray** 灰皿 *haizara*
**Asia** アジア *ajia*
to **ask** 聞きます/頼みます *kikimas/ tanomimas*
**at once** すぐに *suguni*
**author** 作家/作者 *sakka/sakusha*
**automatic** 自動の *jidoh no*
to **avoid** 避けます *sakemas*

**B**

**baby** 赤ちゃん *akachan*
**babysitter** ベビーシッター *bebii shittah*
**back** (*reverse side*) 後ろの/裏の *ushiro no/ura no*
**bad** 悪い *warui*
**bag** 袋/かばん *fukuro/kaban*
**bald** はげた *hageta*
**ball** ボール *bohru*
**ballpoint pen** ボールペン *bohru pen*
**balloon** 風船 *fuusen*
**bamboo** 竹 *take*
» **bamboo shoot** 竹の子 *take no ko*
**bank note** 紙幣 *shihei*
**barber** 床屋/理髪店 *tokoya/rihatsu ten*
**baseball** 野球 *yakyuu*
**bath** (*at home*) 浴室/おふろ *yoku shitsu/ofuro*
» (*public*) 銭湯 *sentoh*
» to **have a bath** おふろに入ります *ofuro ni hairi mas*
**bathroom** (*toilet*) お手洗い/トイレ *o te arai/toire*
**battery** (*torch etc.*) 電池 *denchi*
**beach** 浜/海岸 *hama/kaigan*
**beard** あごひげ *ago hige*
**beautiful** 美しい/きれいな *utsukushii/kireina*
**bed** ベッド *beddo*
**bedroom** 寝室/ベッドルーム *shin shitsu/beddo ruumu*
**bee** 蜂 *hachi*
**before** 前に *mae ni*
to **begin** 始まります/始めます *hajimari mas/majime mas*
» **it begins at 8pm** 八時に始まります *hachiji ni haji mari mas*
**beginner** 初心者/ビギナー *shoshin sha/biginah*
**behind** −の後ろに *-no ushiro ni*
to **believe** 信じます *shinji mas*
**bell** 鐘/ベル *kane/beru*

below 下に/以下の *shita ni/ika no*

belt ベルト *beruto*

best 最高の/一番良い *saikoh no/ichiban ii*

better もっといい *motto ii*

beetle カブトムシ *kabutomushi*

between −の間に *-no aida ni*

bicycle 自転車 *jitensha*

big 大きい *ohkii*

bigger もっと大きい *motto ohkii*

bill 請求書/お勘定 *seikyuu sho/okanjoh*

bin ごみ箱 *gomi bako*
» bin liner ごみ袋 *gomi bukuro*

bird 鳥 *tori*

birthday 誕生日 *tanjohbi*

to bite 噛みます *kamimas*

bitter 苦い *nigai*

black 黒い *kuroi*

blanket 毛布 *mohfu*

bleach 漂白剤 *hyouhaku zai*

to bleed 出血します *shukketsu shimas*

blind 日よけ/ブラインド *hiyoke/buraindo*

blister 水ぶくれ *mizu bukure*

blonde 金髪の/ブロンドの *kinpatsu no/burondo no*

blouse ブラウス *burausu*

blue 青い *aoi*

body 体 *karada*

book 本 *hon*

bookshop 本屋 *honya*

border (frontier) 国境 *kokkyoh*

boring つまらない *tsumaranai*

both 両方の/両方 *ryoh hou no/ryoh hou*

bottle 瓶/ボトル *bin/botoru*

bottle opener 栓抜き *sen nuki*

boy 男の子 *otoko no ko*

boyfriend 彼 *kare*

bra ブラジャー *burajah*

bracelet ブレスレット *buresu retto*

brand 品質/ブランド *hin shitsu/burando*

brand new 新品の *shinpin no*

bread パン *pan*

to break 壊れます/壊します *koware mas/kowashi mas*

to breathe 息をします *iki o shimas*

bride 花嫁 *hana yome*

bridegroom 花婿 *hana muko*

bridge 橋 *hashi*

briefcase ブリーフケース *buriifu keisu*

bright (colour) 鮮やかな *azayaka na*
» (light) 明るい *akarui*

to bring 持って行きます *motte ikimas*

British イギリス人/イギリスの 英国/イギリス *igirisu jin/igirisu no eikoku/igirisu*

broken 壊れた *kowareta*

bronchitis 気管支炎 *kikanshi en*

bronze ブロンズ *buronzu*

brown 茶色の *chairo no*

bruise 傷/あざ *kizu/aza*

brush はけ/ブラシ *hake/burashi*
» (for calligraphy) 筆 *fude*

Buddha 仏陀/ブッダ *budda*

Buddhism 仏教 *bukkyoh*

Buddhist 仏教徒/仏教の *bukkyoh to/bukkyoh no*

buffet バイキング/セルフサービスの *baikingu/serufu sahbisu no*

to build 建てます *tatemas*

building ビル/建物 *biru/tatemono*

bulb (light) 電球 *denkyuu*

burn やけど *yakedo*
» (sunburn) 日焼け *hiyake*

burnt 焼いた/焦げた *yaita/kogeta*

business ビジネス/仕事 *bijinesu/shigoto*
» business card 名刺 *meishi*
» business trip 出張 *shucchoh*

businessman/woman ビジネスマン/女性実業家 *bijinesu man/jyosei jitsugyoh ka*

business person 実業家 *jitsugyoh ka*

**bus station** バス停/バス乗り場 *basu tei/basu noriba*

**busy** 忙しい/混んでいる *isogashii/ kondeiru*

**but** けれども *keredomo*

**button** ボタン *botan*

**to buy** 買います *kaimas*

**by** で *de*

» **by car** 車で *kuruma de*

» **by train** 電車で *densha de*

# C

**calculator** 計算機 *keisanki*

**to call** 呼びます *yobimas*

» **(phone)** 電話をかけます *denwa o kake mas*

**calligraphy** 書道 *shodoh*

**calm** 静かな/落ち着いた *shizukana/ ochitsuita*

**can** (to be able) できます *dekimas*

**can** (tin) 缶/缶詰 *kan/kan zume*

**can opener** 缶切り *kan kiri*

**to cancel** 取り消します/キャンセルします *torikeshi mas/kyanseru shimas*

**cancer** 癌 *gan*

**candle** ろうそく *rohsoku*

**capital** (city) 首都 *shuto*

**career** 職業/経歴 *shoku gyoh/keireki*

**careful** 注意深い *chuui bukai*

**careless** 不注意な *fuchuuina*

**carp** こい *koi*

**carriage** (train) 客車 *kyaku sha*

**cartoon** 漫画 *manga*

**cash** 現金 *genkin*

**cashier** レジ/会計係 *reji/kaikei gakari*

**castle** 城 *shiro*

**cat** 猫 *neko*

**to catch** 捕まえます *tsukamae mas*

» **(train, etc.)** 乗ります *nori mas*

**Catholic** カトリック教徒 *katorikku kyohto*

**CD** CD（シーディー）*shii dii*

» **CD-Rom** CD-Rom（シーディーロム）*shii dii romu*

**celebration** お祝い *oiwai*

**celebrity** 有名人 *yuumeijin*

**central** 中心の *chuushin no*

**centre** 中心 *chuushin*

**century** 世紀 *seiki*

**ceramics** 陶磁器 *tohjiki*

**certificate** 証明書 *shohmeisho*

**chair** いす *isu*

**championship** 選手権 *senshuken*

**change** (coins) おつり/小銭 *otsuri/ kozeni*

**to change** (clothes) 着替えをします *kigae o shimas*

» **(money)** 両替をします *ryohgae o shimas*

» **(trains)** 乗り換えをします *norikae o shimas*

**changing room** 更衣室/試着室 *kohi shitsu/shichaku shitsu*

**character**

» **(personality)** 性格 *seikaku*

» **(written)** 文字 *moji*

**charge** (money) 料金/手数料 *ryoh kin/tesuu ryoh*

**cheap** 安い *yasui*

**to check** 調べます/確認します *shirabe mas/kakunin shimas*

**checkout** (till) レジ *reji*

**Cheers!** 乾杯 *kanpai*

**cherry blossom** 桜 *sakura*

**chess** チェス *chesu*

» **(Japanese)** 将棋 *shohgi*

**chewing gum** （チューイン）ガム *(chuu in) gamu*

**child** 子供 *kodomo*

**children** 子供たち *kodomo tachi*

**China** 中国 *chuugoku*

**Chinese** (language) 中国語 *chuugoku go*

» **(people)** 中国人 *chuugoku jin*

**chips** (French fries) フライドポテト *furaido poteto*

**chocolate** チョコレート *chokoreito*

**to choose** 選びます *erabimas*

chopsticks はし *hashi*

» chopsticks rest はし置き *hashi oki*

Christian キリスト教徒 *kirisuto kyohto*

church 教会 *kyohkai*

cicada セミ *semi*

cigar 葉巻 *hamaki*

cigarette タバコ *tabako*

cinema 映画館 *eigakan*

circle 円/輪 *en/wa*

circus サーカス *sahkasu*

city 市/町 *shi/machi*

classical 古典的な *kotenteki na*

» classical music クラシック音楽 *kurrashikku ongaku*

claustrophobia 閉所恐怖症 *heisho kyoufu shoh*

clean きれいな/清潔な *kirei na/ seiketsu na*

clever 利口な/賢い *rikoh na/kashikoi*

client 顧客/お得意様 *kokyaku/otokui sama*

climate 気候 *kikoh*

to climb 登ります *noborimas*

cloakroom クローク/手荷物預かり所 *kurohku/tenimotsu azukari jo*

clock 時計 *tokei*

close (by) 近くに *chikaku ni*

to close 閉めます/終わります *shime mas/owarimas*

closed 閉店/休館 *heiten/kyuukan*

clothes 洋服/衣類 *youfuku/irui*

cloudy 曇った *kumotta*

coach (person) コーチ/指導者 *koh chi/shidoh sha*

» (vehicle) 大型/長距離バス *oh gata/choh kyori basu*

coast 海岸 *kaigan*

coat-hanger ハンガー *hangah*

cockroach ごきぶり *gokiburi*

cocktail カクテル *kakuteru*

coin 硬貨/小銭 *kohka/kozeni*

cold 寒い/冷たい *samui/tsumetai*

» to have a cold 風邪をひいています *kaze o hiite imas*

colleague 同僚 *dohryoh*

college 大学 *daigaku*

colour 色 *iro*

comb くし *kushi*

to come 来ます *kimas*

come in! どうぞ *dohzo*

comfortable 快適な/心地いい *kaiteki na/kokochi ii*

to commute (to work) 通勤します *tsuukin shimas*

Company (business) 会社 *kaisha*

compared with と比べて *to kurabete*

to complain 文句を言います *monku o ii mas*

» complaint 文句/苦情 *monku/kujoh*

complete 完全な *kanzenna*

complicated 複雑な *fuku zatsu na*

to compromise 妥協します *dakyoh shimas*

compulsory 必修の/強制的な *hisshuu no/kyohsei teki na*

composer 作曲家 *sakkyokuka*

computer (laptop) ノートパソコン コンピューター *nohto pasokon conpyuutah*

conference 会議/協議会 *kaigi/kyoh gikai*

to confirm 確認します *kakunin shimas*

conjunctivitis 結膜炎 *ketsumaku en*

conservation 保存/維持 *hozon/iji*

conservative 保守的な *hoshu teki na*

to contact 連絡します *renraku shimas*

contagious 伝染性の *densen sei no*

continent 大陸 *tairiku*

contraceptive 避妊薬/避妊具 *hinin yaku/hiningu*

contract 契約 *keiyaku*

to continue 続けます/続きます *tsuzuke mas/tsuzuki mas*

convenient 便利な/都合の良い *benri na/tsugoh no ii*

conversation 会話 *kaiwa*

**to convey** 運びます/伝えます *hakobi mas/tsutae mas*

**to cook** 料理をします *ryohri o shimas*
  » **cooked** 調理済みの *chohri zumi no*

**cool** 涼しい/冷たい *suzushii/tsume tai*

**corkscrew** コルク抜き/スクリュー *koruku nuki/sukuryuu*

**corner** 曲がり角 *magarikado*

**correct** 正しい *tadashii*

**cosmetics** 化粧品 *keshoh hin*

**to cost** かかります *kakari mas*

**cotton** (material) 綿/コットン *men/kotton*
  » (thread) 木綿糸 *momen ito*

**cotton wool** 脱脂綿 *dasshimen*

**to cough** 咳をします *seki o shimas*

**to count** 数えます *kazoe mas*

**country** (nation) 国 *kuni*

**countryside** 田舎/地方 *inaka/chihoh*

**couple** (pair) 一組 *hitokumi*
  » (people) カップル/アベック *kappuru/abekku*

**course** (lessons) コース/課程 *kohsu/katei*

**court** (law) 裁判所 *saibansho*
  » (tennis) コート *kohto*

**cram school** 塾/予備校 *juku/yobi koh*

**crisps** ポテトチップス *poteto chippusu*

**crossing** (junction) 交差点 *kohsaten*

**crossroad** 十字路 *juujiro*

**crowd** 人込み *hitogomi*

**crowded** 混雑した *konzatsu shita*

**cruise** 船旅 *funa tabi*

**crutch** 松葉づえ *matsuba zue*

**to cry** 泣きます *nakimas*

**culture** 文化 *bunka*

**cup** 茶碗/カップ *chawan/kappu*

**curry** カレー *karei*

**current** (electricity) 電流 *denryuu*

**cushion** クッション *kusshon*
  » (on a tatami mat) 座布団 *zabuton*

**custom** 習慣 *shuukan*

**customs** 税関/関税 *zeikan/kanzei*

**customer** 顧客/客 *kokyaku/kyaku*

**cut** (wound) 傷口 *kizu guchi*

**to cut** 切ります *kiri mas*
  » **to cut oneself** 怪我をします *kega o shimas*

**cute** かわいい *kawaii*

**cycling** サイクリング *saikuringu*

**cyclist** サイクリスト *saikurisuto*

**daily** 毎日の/日々の *mainichi no/hibi no*

**dairy products** 乳製品 *nyuu seihin*

**damage** 損害/ダメージ *songai/dameiji*

**damp** 湿気/湿った *shikke/shimetta*

**dance** 踊り/ダンス *odori/dansu*

**to dance** 踊ります/ダンスをします *odori mas/dansu o shimas*

**danger** 危険 *kiken*

**dangerous** 危険な *kiken na*

**dark** 暗い *kurai*

**day** 日/日にち *hi/hi nichi*
  » **day after tomorrow** あさって *asatte*
  » **day before yesterday** おととい *ototoi*

**dead** 死んだ/亡くなった *shinda/nakunatta*

**deaf** 耳の聞こえない *mimi no kikoe nai*

**dear** (expensive) 高価な *kohka na*
  » (loved) いとしい/愛する *itoshii/ai suru*

**deep** 深い *fukai*

**deer** しか *shika*

**definitely** 確かに *tashika ni*
  » (as a reply) その通りです。 *sono tohri des*

**degree** (temperature) 度 *do*
  » (university) 学位 *gakui*

**delay** 遅れ *okure*

**delicate** 繊細な *sensaina*

delicious おいしい *oishii*

delighted 喜んでいる *yorokonde iru*

to deliver 配達します *haitatsu shimas*

›› *(to give birth)* 出産します *shussan shimas*

to depart 出発します *shuppatsu shimas*

department *(in shop)* 売り場 *uriba*

›› *(at university)* 学部 *gakubu*

department store デパート/百貨店 *depahto/hyakkaten*

deposit 預金 *yokin*

to describe 述べます/表現します *nobe mas/hyohgen shimas*

destination 目的地/行き先 *mokuteki chi/ikisaki*

to develop 発達します/開発します *hattatsu shimas/kaihatsu shimas*

›› *(film)* 現像します *genzoh shimas*

diabetes 糖尿病 *tohnyoh byoh*

to dial 電話をかけます/ダイヤルします *denwa o kakemas/daiyaru shimas*

dialect 方言 *hohgen*

dialling tone 発信音 *hasshin on*

diamond ダイヤモンド *daiya mondo*

diary 日記/手帳 *nikki/techoh*

dice さいころ *saikoro*

dictionary 辞書 *jisho*

to die 死にます *shini mas*

Diet *(Japanese parliament)* 国会 *kokkai*

different 異なった/違った *koto natta/chigatta*

difficult 難しい *muzukashii*

digital camera デジタルカメラ *deji taru kamera*

diplomat 外交官 *gaikoh kan*

directory 名簿 *meibo*

›› *(telephone)* 電話帳 *denwa choh*

dirty 汚い *kitanai*

disabled 体の不自由な *karadano fujiyuu na*

›› *(disabled people)* 体の不自由な人 *karadano fujiyuu na hito*

disappointment 失望 *shitsu boh*

disc *(computer)* ディスク *disuku*

disco ディスコ *disuko*

discount 割引 *waribiki*

to discover 発見します/見つけます *hakken shimas/mitsukemas*

dish *(container)* お皿 *osara*

›› *(cooked)* 料理 *ryohri*

to dislike 嫌いです *kirai des*

dislocation *(bone)* 脱臼 *dakkyuu*

disposable 使い捨て *tsukai sute*

›› disposable camera 使い捨てカメラ *tsukai sute kamera*

›› disposable nappies 紙おむつ *kami omutsu*

distance 距離/間隔 *kyori/kankaku*

divorce/d 離婚/離婚した *rikon/rikon shita*

to do します/行います *shimas/okonai mas*

document 書類 *shorui*

dog 犬 *inu*

doll 人形 *ningyoh*

dollar ドル *doru*

domestic 家庭の *katei no*

›› *(national)* 国内の *kokunai no*

door ドア *doa*

›› *(Japanese sliding doors)* 障子/ふすま *shohji/fusuma*

down 下へ *shita e*

download ダウンロード *daunrohdo*

downstairs 下の階/階下 *shita no kai/kai ka*

drama 演劇/ドラマ *engeki/dorama*

to draw *(a picture/map)* 描きます *kaki mas*

›› *(a line)* 引きます *hikimas*

dream 夢 *yume*

drink 飲み物/ドリンク *nomimono/dorinku*

to drink 飲みます *nomi mas*

to drive 運転します *unten shimas*

drug addict 麻薬常用者 *mayaku johyoh sha*

**dry-cleaner** クリーニング屋 *kurii
    ningu ya*
**dust** ほこり *hokori*
**duvet** 羽毛布団 *umoh buton*
**DVD-player** DVDプレーヤー *dii bui
    dii purei yah*

# E

**each** それぞれの *sore zore no*
**early** 早い/早く *hayai/hayaku*
**earth** (planet) 地球 *chikyuu*
  » (soil) 土 *tsuchi*
**earthquake** 地震 *jishin*
**east** 東 *higashi*
**Eastern** 東の *higashi no*
**easy** 簡単な *kantan na*
to **eat** 食べます *tabe mas*
**economy** 経済 *keizai*
**edible** 食べられる *taberareru*
**education** 教育 *kyoh iku*
**either... or...** …かまたは… *…ka
    mata wa...*
**election** 選挙 *senkyo*
**electricity** 電気/電力 *denki/denryoku*
**email** メール *meiru*
to **email** メールを送ります *meiru o
    okuri mas*
**embarrassment** 困惑 *konwaku*
**embassy** 大使館 *taishikan*
**emergency** 緊急事態 *kinkyuu jitai*
**emperor** 天皇 *ten noh*
**empress** 皇后 *kohgoh*
**employee** 従業員 *juu gyoo in*
**empty** 空の/空いている *kara
    no/aiteiru*
to **empty** 空にします *kara ni shimas*
**end** 終わり *owari*
**endurance** 我慢 *gaman*
**engaged** (to be married) 婚約中 *kon
    yaku chuu*
  » (telephone) 話し中 *hanashi chuu*
**England** (and UK) イギリス *igirisu*
**English** (and British) イギリス人
    *igirisu jin*

  » (language) 英語 *eigo*
to **enjoy** 楽しみます *tanoshimi mas*
**enjoyable** 楽しい *tanoshii*
**enough** 十分な *juubun na*
to **enter** 入ります *hairimas*
**entertainment** 娯楽/催し物 *goraku/
    moyohshi mono*
**entrance** 入口 *iriguchi*
**envelope** 封筒 *fuutoh*
**environment** 環境 *kankyoh*
**environmentally friendly** 環境にやさ
    しい *kankyoh ni yasashii*
**essential** 絶対必要な *zettai hitsu
    yohna*
**estate agent** 不動産屋 *fudohsan ya*
**estimate** 見積り *mitsumori*
**Europe** ヨーロッパ *yohroppa*
**even** (not odd) 偶数の *guusuu no*
**evening** 夕方/晩 *yuugata/ban*
**event** 行事/出来事 *gyohji/dekigoto*
**everyone** みんな/だれでも *minna/
    dare demo*
**everything** 何もかも *nanimo kamo*
**everywhere** どこでも *doko demo*
**exactly** その通りです *sono tohri des*
**examination** 試験/検査 *shiken/kensa*
**example** 例 *rei*
  » for example 例えば *tatoeba*
**excellent** 素晴らしい *subarashii*
to **exchange** 交換します *kohkan shimas*
  » (money) 両替をします *ryohgae o
    shimas*
**exchange rate** 為替レート *kawase
    reito*
**excited** わくわくした *waku waku
    shita*
**exciting** おもしろい *omoshiroi*
to **excuse** 許します *yurushimas*
**executive** 重役 *juuyaku*
**exercise** 運動 *undoh*
**exhibition** 展覧会/博覧会 *tenran
    kai/hakuran kai*
**expensive** 高い/高価な *takai/koh
    kana*

**experience** 経験 *keiken*

**experiment** 実験 *jikken*

**expert** 専門家 *senmonka*

to **explain** 説明します *setsumei shimas*

**explosion** 爆発 *bakuhatsu*

**export** 輸出 *yushutsu*

to **export** 輸出します *yushutsu shimas*

to **express** 表現します *hyohgen shimas*

**external** 外部の *gaibu no*

to **extinguish** 消します *keshi mas*

**extra** 追加の/余分な *tsuika no/ yobun na*

» *(charge)* 追加料金/別料金 *tsuika ryohkin/betsu ryohkin*

## F

**factory** 工場 *kohjoh*

to **fail** 失敗します *shippai shimas*

» *(exam)* (試験に) 落ちます *(shiken ni) ochimas*

to **faint** 気絶します *kizetsu shimas*

**fair** *(just)* 公平な *koh hei na*

**fair** *(haired)* 金髪の *kinpatsu no*

**fairly** 公平に *koh hei ni*

**fake** にせ物 *nise mono*

to **fall** 落ちます *ochimas*

**false** 間違った *machi gatta*

**familiar** 良く知っている *yoku shitte iru*

**family** 家族 *kazoku*

**famous** 有名な *yuumei na*

**fan** うちわ/扇子 *uchiwa/sensu*

» *(electric)* 扇風機 *senpuuki*

» *(supporter)* ファン *fan*

**far** *(away)* 遠くに *tohkuni*

**fare** 運賃 *unchin*

**farm** 農場 *nohjoh*

**farmer** 農家の人 *nohka no hito*

**fashion** ファッション/流行 *fasshion/ ryuukoh*

**fast** 速い *hayai*

**fat** 太った *futotta*

**fatal** 致命的な *chimei teki na*

**father** 父 *chichi*

» *(another person's)* お父さん *otoh san*

**faulty** 欠陥のある *kekkan no aru*

**favourite** 好きな *sukina*

**feather** 羽 *hane*

to **feed** 物を食べさせます *mono o tabe sase mas*

» *(animals)* 餌をやります *esa o yarimas*

to **feel** 感じます *kanji mas*

» *(ill/well)* 気分が悪いです/気分が 良いです *kibun ga warui des/kibun ga ii des*

**feeling** 気持ち/感じ *kimochi/kanji*

**female** 女性/婦人 *josei/fujin*

**feminine** 女らしい *onna rashii*

**fever** 熱 *netsu*

**few** 少しの *sukoshino*

» **a few** 多少の *tashoh no*

**fiancé(e)** 婚約者 *konyakusha*

**field** 野原 *nohara*

» *(for sport)* 競技場 *kyohgi joh*

**file** *(documents)* ファイル *fairu*

» *(computer)* ファイル *fairu*

» *(nail)* やすり *yasuri*

**film** 映画 *eiga*

**finance** 財政 *zaisei*

to **find** 見つけます *mitsuke mas*

**fine** *(OK)* いい/大丈夫な *ii/dai johbu na*

» *(penalty)* 罰金 *bakkin*

» *(weather)* 晴れた *hareta*

to **finish** 終わります *owarimas*

**fire** 火/火事 *hi/kaji*

**fire brigade** 消防所 *shohboh sho*

**fire extinguisher** 消火器 *shohkaki*

**fireworks** 花火 *hanabi*

**firm** 固い *katai*

» *(company)* 会社 *kaisha*

**first** 一番の/最初の *ichiban no/sai sho no*

» **first aid** 応急手当 *ohkyuu teate*

to **fix** *(mend)* 直します *naoshimas*

**flag** 旗 *hata*

flammable 燃えやすい moeyasui

flash (camera) フラッシュ furasshu

flat (apartment) アパート/マンション apahto/manshon

» (level) 平らな tairana

flavour 味 aji

flight フライト/飛行 furaito/hikoh

flood 洪水 kohzui

floor 床 yuka

» (storey) 階 kai

flour 小麦粉 komugiko

flower 花 hana

fluent 流暢な ryuuchoh na

fly (insect) はえ hae

to fly 飛びます tobimas

foggy 霧の深い kiri no fukai

foil アルミホイル arumi hoiru

folk music 民謡 min yoh

to follow ついて行きます/続きます tsuite iki mas/tsuzuki mas

following (next) 次の tsugi no

food 食べ物 tabe mono

food poisoning 食中毒 shoku chuu doku

foot 足 ashi

» on foot 歩いて aruite

football サッカー sakkah

footpath 小道 komichi

for のために no tame ni

forbidden 禁じられた kinjirareta

foreign 外国の gaikoku no

» foreign language 外国語 gaikoku go

foreigner 外国人 gaikoku jin

forest 森 mori

to forget 忘れます wasuremas

to forgive 許します yurushimas

fork フォーク fohku

formal 正式の seishiki no

forward 前へ mae e

fox きつね kitsune

foyer 玄関 genkan

» (at a hotel) ロビー robii

fragile 壊れやすい koware yasui

free 自由な jiyuu na

» (at leisure) 暇な hima na

» (unoccupied) 空いている aiteiru

French フランス語/フランスの furan su go/furan su no

frequently 何度も/頻繁に nandomo/hinpanni

fresh 新鮮な shinsen na

fried 油で揚げた abura de ageta

friend 友人/友達 yuujin/tomodachi

friendly 好意的な kohi teki na

to frighten 驚かせます odoro kase mas

from から kara

front 前 mae

» in front of -の前に -no mae ni

frozen food 冷凍食品 reitoh shokuhin

fruit 果物 kuda mono

to fry 炒めます itame mas

» to deep-fry 油で揚げます abura de agemas

fuel 燃料 nenryoh

full いっぱいの ippai no

» (stomach) お腹がいっぱいです onaka ga ippai des

fun 楽しみ tanoshimi

» to have fun 楽しみます tanoshimi mas

funeral 葬式/葬儀 sohshiki/sohgi

funny (amazing) 滑稽な kokkei na

» (peculiar) 変な hen na

fur 毛皮 kegawa

furniture 家具 kagu

future 将来/未来 shoh rai/mirai

# G

to gamble 賭け事をします kake goto o shimas

game (match) 試合 shiai

gangster やくざ yakuza

garden 庭 niwa

» Japanese garden 日本庭園 nihon teien

» beer garden ビアガーデン bia gah den

gateway to a shrine 鳥居 torii

generous 気前の良い kimae no ii

gentleman/men 男性/紳士 dan sei/shinshi

genuine 本物の honmono no

geography 地理 chiri

to get 手に入れます te ni ire mas

» to get off 降ります orimas

» to get on 乗ります norimas

girl 女の子 onna no ko

girlfriend 彼女 kanojo

to give あげます agemas

» to give back 返します kaeshimas

glass (in windows) ガラス garasu

» (container) コップ/グラス koppu/gurasu

glasses 眼鏡 megane

global warming 地球温暖化 chikyuu ondanka

to go 行きます ikimas

» to go away 立ち去ります tachisari mas

» to go in 入ります hairimas

god 神 kami

gold 金/ゴールド kin/gohrudo

» (colour) 金色 kiniro

golf ゴルフ gorufu

» golf club ゴルフクラブ gorufu kurabu

» golf course ゴルフコース gorufu kohsu

good 良い ii

» to be good at 上手です johzu des

gorge 峡谷 kei koku

government 政府 seifu

» (cabinet) 内閣 naikaku

to graduate 卒業します sotsugyoh shimas

graduation ceremony 卒業式 sotsu gyohshiki

grammar 文法 bunpoh

grandparents 祖父母 sofubo

grapefruit グレープフルーツ gureipu furuutsu

grave お墓 o haka

great 大きな ohkina

» Great Buddha 大仏 dai butsu

green 緑地 ryokuchi

» (colour) 緑色 midori iro

to greet 挨拶をします/むかえます aisatsu o shimas/mukaemas

grey 灰色/グレー hai iro/gurei

grilled 焼いた yaita

guest 客/来賓 kyaku/raihin

guide (person) ガイド gaido

» guided tour ガイド付きツアー gaido tsuki tsuah

guidebook ガイドブック gaido bukku

guilty 有罪の/うしろめたい yuuzai no/ushirometai

guitar ギター gitah

gun 銃 juu

gymnasium 体育館 taiikukan

» (for martial arts) 道場 dohjoh

## H

hair 髪の毛/毛 kami no ke/ke

hairbrush ヘアブラシ hea burashi

hairdresser 美容師 biyohshi

hairdryer ヘアドライヤー hea doraiyah

half 半分 hanbun

half an hour 三十分 san juppun

hand bag 鞄/ハンドバッグ kaban/hando baggu

hand made 手作りの tezukuri no

handkerchief ハンカチ hankachi

handle 取っ手 totte

hangover 二日酔い futsukayoi

happy 幸せな/うれしい shiawase na/ureshii

hard 固い katai

» (difficult) 難しい muzukashii

hard drive ハードドライブ hahdo doraibu

harmful 有害な yuugai na

to hate 憎みます nikumi mas

**to have** あります/持っています *ari mas/motte imass*

**hay fever** 花粉症 *kafun shoh*

**he** 彼は/が *kare wa/ga*

**health** 健康 *kenkoh*

» **health food** 健康食品 *ken koh shoku hin*

**healthy** 健康な *kenkoh na*

**to hear** 聞きます *kikimas*

**heat** 熱/暑さ *netsu/atsusa*

**heater** 暖房/ヒーター *danboh/hiitah*

**heavy** 重い *omoi*

**height** 高さ *takasa*

» **(of a person)** 身長 *shinchoh*

**help** 助け *tasuke*

**to help** 助けます/手伝います *tasuke mas/tetsudaimas*

**her** 彼女に/彼女の *kanojo ni/kanojo no*

**here** ここに/で *kokoni/de*

» **here is** ここにあります *kokoni arimas*

**high** 高い *takai*

» **high chair** 子供用のいす *kodomo yoh no isu*

**high school** 高等学校/高校 *kohtoh gakkoh/kohkoh*

» **high school students** 高校生 *kohkoh sei*

**hiking** ハイキング *haikingu*

**him** 彼に/を *kare ni/o*

**to hire** 借ります *karimas*

**his** 彼の *kare no*

**history** 歴史 *rekishi*

**HIV** エイズウイルス *eizu uirusu*

» **HIV positive** エイズウイルスに感染した *eizu uirusu ni kansen shita*

**hobby** 趣味 *shumi*

**to hold** 持ちます/つかみます *mochi mas/tsukami mas*

**holiday** 休暇 *kyuuka*

» **on holiday** 休暇で *kyuuka de*

» **national holiday** 祝日/祭日 *shuku jitsu/saijitsu*

**to be homesick** ホームシックです *hohmu shikku des*

**homosexual** 同性愛の *dohsei ai no*

» **(a person)** 同性愛者 *dohsei ai sha*

**honest** 正直な *shohjiki na*

**honeymoon** 新婚旅行 *shin kon ryokoh*

**to hope** 望みます/願います *nozomi mas/negaimas*

» **I hope so** そうだといいです *soh dato ii des*

**horrible** 恐ろしい *osoro shii*

**horror** 恐怖 *kyofu*

» **horror film** ホラー映画 *horah eiga*

**horse** 馬 *uma*

» **horse racing** 競馬 *keiba*

» **horse riding** 乗馬 *johba*

**hospital** 病院 *byohin*

**hospitality** 歓待/手厚いもてなし *kantai/teatsui motenashi*

**hot** 熱い *atsui*

» **(weather)** 暑い *atsui*

» **(spicy)** 辛い *karai*

**hour** 時間 *jikan*

**house** 家 *ie*

**housework** 家事 *kaji*

**how** どう/どうやって *doh/doh yatte*

» **how far?** 距離はどのくらいですか? *kyori wa dono kurai des ka*

» **how many?** いくつですか *ikutsu des ka*

» **how much does it cost?** いくらかかりますか? *ikura kakari mas ka*

**human** 人間の *ningen no*

» **human being** 人間 *ningen*

**humane** 慈悲深い *jihi bukai*

**humble** 控え目な *hikaeme na*

**humid and hot** 蒸し暑い *mushi atsui*

**humour** ユーモア *yuumoa*

**to be hungry** お腹がすいています *onaka ga suite imas*

**to hurry** 急ぎます *isogimas*

**in a hurry** 急いで *isoide*

**to hurt** 傷つけます *kizu tsuke mas*

» **it hurts** 痛みます *itami mas*

husband 夫 otto
» (another person's) ご主人 goshujin

**I**

I 私は/が watashi wa/ga
ice 氷 kohri
ice cube 氷 kohri
ice rink アイススケート場 aisu sukeito joh
iced 氷で冷やした kohri de hiya shita
iced coffee/tea アイスコーヒー/ティー aisu koh hii/tii
idea 考え kangae
if... もし…なら moshi ...nara
illness 病気 byohki
immediately すぐに suguni
important 重要な juuyoh na
impossible 不可能な fukanoh na
in ~の中に ~no naka ni
» in front of ~の前に ~no mae ni
» in order to ~するために ~suru tame ni
inconvenient 不便な fuben na
incorrect 間違った machigatta
to include 含みます fukumimas
independent 独立した dokuritsu shita
indoor 室内の shitsunai no
industry 産業 sangyoh
infamous 評判の悪い hyohban no warui
infection 感染 kansen
informal 非公式の hikohshikino
information 情報 Johhoh
injection 注射 chuusha
to injure (someone) けがをさせます kega o sase mas
» injured 傷ついた kizu tsuita
innocent 無邪気な mujaki na
» (legal) 無実の mujitsu no
insect 虫 mushi
» insect bite 虫刺され mushi sasare
» insect repellent 防虫剤 bohchuu zai
inside ~の内側に ~no uchi gawa ni

insulin インシュリン inshurin
insult 侮辱 bujoku
insurance 保険 hoken
» insurance policy 保険証券 hoken shohken
intelligent 知的な/頭がいい chiteki na/atama ga ii
interesting おもしろい omoshiroi
international 国際的な kokusaiteki na
internationalisation 国際化 kokusai ka
internet インターネット intahnetto
» internet connection インターネット接続 intahnetto setsuzoku
to interpret 通訳します tsuuyaku shimas
interpreter 通訳者 tsuuyakusha
interval (theatre etc.) 休憩 kyuukei
into ~の中に ~no naka ni
to introduce 紹介します shohkai shimas
invitation 招待 shohtai
Ireland アイルランド airurando
Irish (people) アイルランド人 airurando jin
iron (metal) 鉄 tetsu
» (for clothes) アイロン airon
is there...? …はありますか? wa arimas ka
island 島 shima
isolated 孤立した koritsu shita
it それ sore wa/ga
itchy かゆい kayu i

**J**

Japan 日本 nihon
» Japan Sea 日本海 nihon kai
Japanese (people) 日本人 nihon jin
» language 日本語 nihon go
jellyfish くらげ kurage
job 仕事 shigoto
joke 冗談 johdan
journalist 報道記者/ジャーナリスト hohdoh kisha/jahnarisuto
journey 旅行 ryokoh
jumper セーター seitah

## K

key 鍵 kagi
  » key ring キーホルダー kii horudah
to kill 殺します koroshi mas
kind 親切な shinsetsu na
  » (sort) 種類 shurui
king 王 oh
to kiss キスをします kisu o shimas
kite たこ tako
to kneel ひざまずきます hizamazuki mas
  » (formally on tatami) 正座します seiza shimas
knife ナイフ naifu
to knock (door) ノックします nokku shimas
to know 知っています shitte imas
  » I don't know わかりません wakari masen
knowledge 知識 chishiki
Korea 韓国 kankoku
Korean (language) 韓国語 kankokugo
  » (people) 韓国人 kankokujin

## L

lady 女性/女の人 josei/ onna no hito
lager ラガービール ragah biiru
lake 湖 mizuumi
language 言語/言葉 gengo/kotoba
laptop ノートパソコン nohto pasokon
large 大きい ohkii
last 最後の saigo no
late 遅い osoi
later 後で atode
to laugh 笑います waraimas
launderette コインランドリー koin randorii
laundry 洗濯物 sentakumono
law 法律 hohritsu
lawyer 弁護士 bengoshi
lazy 怠惰な taida na
to learn 習います naraimas
to leave (go away) 去ります sarimas
  » (forget sthg.) 置き忘れます okiwasure mas

left 左 hidari
length 長さ nagasa
lens (camera) レンズ renzu
  » (contact) コンタクトレンズ kontakuto renzu
lesson 授業 jugyoh
letter 手紙 tegami
  » (of alphabet) 文字 moji
library 図書館 toshokan
licence 免許 menkyo
  » (driving) 運転免許証 unten menkyo shoh
lie うそ uso
to lie down 横になります yoko ni nari mas
life 命/一生 inochi/isshoh
lifeboat 救命ボート kyuumei bohto
lifeguard 監視員 kanshiin
lifejacket 救命胴衣 kyuumei dohi
to lift 持ち上げます mochiage mas
light ライト/光 raito/hikari
  » light bulb 電球 denkyuu
light (colour) 明るい akarui
  » (weight) 軽い karui
lighter ライター raitah
lightning 稲妻 inazuma
to like 好きです sukides
  » to like doing something するのが好きです surunoga suki des
limited 限られた kagirareta
line 線 sen
lipstick 口紅 kuchibeni
liquid 液体 ekitai
to listen (to) 聞きます kikimas
litter ごみ gomi
little 小さい chiisai
  » a little 少しの sukoshi no
to live 住みます sumimas
local 地方の chihoh no
to lock 錠をかけます kagi o kake mas
locker ロッカー rokkah
long 長い nagai
long-distance 長距離 chohkyori
  » long-distance call 長距離電話 chohkyori denwa

to look (at) 見ます *mimas*
to look after 面倒を見ます *mendoh o mimas*
to look for 探します *sagashimas*
  lost 道に迷った *michi ni mayotta*
  a lot (of) たくさん *takusan*
  loud うるさい *urusai*
to love 愛します *aishimas*
  low 低い *hikui*
  low-fat 低脂肪の *teishiboh no*
  lucky 幸運な *kohun na*
  » lucky charm お守り *omamori*
  luggage 手荷物 *tenimotsu*
  lunch box 弁当 *bentoh*

## M

  magazine 雑誌 *zasshi*
to make 作ります *tsukurimas*
  male 男性の *danseino*
  man/men 男/男の人 *otoko/ otokonohito*
  many 多くの *ohkuno*
  map 地図 *chizu*
  maple tree かえで *kaede*
  marathon マラソン *marason*
  market 市場 *ichiba*
  marriage 結婚 *kekkon*
  married 結婚した *kekkonshita*
  » to get married 結婚します *kekkon shimas*
  martial arts 武道/武術 *budoh/ bujutsu*
  massage マッサージ *massahji*
  match (game) 試合 *shiai*
  material 材料 *zairyoh*
  mathematics 数学 *suugaku*
to matter 重要です *juuyoh des*
  » it doesn't matter 気にしないで下さ *ki ni shinai de kudasai*
  » what's the matter? どうかしましたか? *doh ka shimashita ka*
  mattress マットレス *mattoresu*
  » (Japanese style mattress) 敷布団 *shiki buton*

  me 私に/を *watashi ni/o*
  meal 食事 *shokuji*
to mean 意味します *imishimas*
  » what does this mean? これはどういう意味ですか *kore wa doh iu imi des ka*
  meat 肉 *niku*
  medical 医学の *igaku no*
  medicine 薬 *kusuri*
  Mediterranean sea 地中海 *chichuu kai*
  medium (size) 中ぐらい *chuugurai*
  » (steak) ミディアム *midiamu*
  meeting 会議 *kaigi*
  memory 記憶 *kioku*
  memory card メモリーカード *memorii kahdo*
  message 伝言 *dengon*
  microwave oven 電子レンジ *denshi renji*
  midday 正午 *shohgo*
  middle 真ん中 *mannaka*
  middle-aged 中年の *chuunen no*
  midnight 真夜中 *mayonaka*
  mild 温和な *onwana*
  milk 牛乳/ミルク *gyuu nyuu/miruku*
to mind 気にします *ki ni shimas*
  » do you mind if ...? …してもいいですか? *...shitemo ii des ka*
  » I don't mind どうぞ *doh zo*
  minister 大臣 *daijin*
  mirror 鏡 *kagami*
to miss (bus etc.) 乗り遅れます *noriokuremas*
  » (nostalgia) 寂しいです *sabishii des*
  mistake 間違い *machigai*
  mobile phone 携帯電話 *keitai denwa*
  model モデル *moderu*
  modem モデム *modemu*
  modern 現代の *gendai no*
  moment 瞬間 *shunkan*
  money お金 *okane*
  monthly 月々の *tsukizuki no*

monument 記念建造物/記念碑 kinen kenzohbutsu/kinenhi

moon 月 tsuki

more もっと motto

morning 朝 asa

mosquito 蚊 ka

most (of) ほとんどの hotondono

mother 母 haha

» (another person's) お母さん okah san

motorway 高速道路 kohsoku dohro

mountain 山 yama

moustache 口ひげ kuchi hige

MP3-player MP3 (エムスリー)プレイヤー emu pii suriii pureiyah

museum 博物館 hakubutsukan

music 音楽 ongaku

musical instrument 楽器 gakki

» Japanese harp 琴 koto

» Japanese-style guitar 三味線 shamisen

mustard からし/マスタード karashi/masutahdo

my 私の watashi no

## N

nail clippers/scissors 爪切り tsume kiri

nail file 爪やすり tsume yasuri

nail polish マニキュア manikyua

nail polish remover 除光液 jokoheki

naked 裸の hadaka no

name 名前 namae

» surname 姓/名字 sei/myohji

» my name is... 私の名前は…です watashi no namae wa ... des

» what is your name? お名前は？ o namae wa…

napkin (テーブル) ナプキン (tei buru) napukin

nappy おむつ omutsu

» disposable nappy 紙おむつ kami omutsu

narrow 狭い semai

national 国の kuni no

nationality 国籍 kokuseki

natural 自然の shizen no

nausea 吐き気 hakike

navy 海軍 kaigun

navy blue 紺色の konirono

near 近い chikai

» nearest 一番近い ichi ban chikai

to need 必要です/～がいります hitsuyoh des/~ga irimas

neighbour 近所の人 kinjo hito ho

neither ... nor... …も…もない ...mo …mo nai

nervous 神経質な/ドキドキして shin kei shitsu na/dokidoki shite

never 決して…ない/一度もありません kesshite ... nai/ichidomo arimasen

new 新しい atarashii

» New Year 新年 shinnen

» New Year's Day 元日 ganjitsu

» New Year's Eve 大晦日 ohmisoka

» New Year's card 年賀状 nengajoh

news ニュース nyuusu

newspaper 新聞 shinbun

next 次の tsugi no

» week/month/year 来週/来月/来年 raishuu/raigetsu/rainen

next to ～の隣に ~no tonari ni

nice 素敵な suteki na

night 夜 yoru

no いいえ iie

nobody 誰も…ない daremo ... nai

noise 音 oto

noisy うるさい urusai

non-smoking 禁煙 kinen

» non-smoking car 禁煙車 kinensha

» non-smoking seat 禁煙席 kinen seki

normal 普通の futsuu no

north 北 kita

note (bank) 紙幣 shihei

nothing 何も…ない nani mo ... nai

now 今 ima

nowhere どこにも…ない *doko nimo … nai*

nuclear power 原子力 *genshiryoku*

number 数/番号 *kazu/bangoh*

» *(even)* 偶数 *guusuu*

» *(odd)* 奇数 *kisuu*

## O

occupied *(seat, toilet)* 使用中 *shiyoh chuu*

of ... …の … *no*

of course もちろん *mochiron*

off *(TV, light)* 止まって *tomatte*

» *(milk)* 腐った *kusatta*

office 職場 *shokuba*

official 公式の *kohshiki no*

often よく *yoku*

» how often? どのくらい頻繁に…ですか? *donokurai hinpanni …des ka*

OK 了解/大丈夫 *ryoh kai/daijohbu*

old *(object)* 古い *furui*

» *(person)* 年をとった *toshi o totta*

old-fashioned 時代遅れの *jidai okure no*

Olympic オリンピック *orinpikku*

on ~の上に *~no ue ni*

once 一度 *ichido*

only 唯一の/~だけ *yuiitsu no/~dake*

open 開いている *aiteiru*

to open 開きます/開けます *hirakimas/akemes*

operation 手術 *shujutsu*

opinion 意見 *iken*

» in my opinion 私の考えでは… *watashi no kangae dewa…*

opposite 反対側に *hantai gawa ni*

optician 眼鏡屋 *megane ya*

or か、または *ka, mata wa*

orange *(colour)* オレンジ色 *orenji iro*

to order *(food)* 注文します *chuumon shimas*

to organise *(a plan)* 準備します *junbi shimas*

original 最初の *saisho no*

our 私たちの *watashi tachi no*

ours 私たちのもの *watashi tachi no mono*

out 外に *soto ni*

» out of order 故障中 *koshoh chuu*

outdoor/s 屋外の/で *okugai no/de*

outside ... …の外に … *no soto ni*

over ~の上に *~no ue ni*

owner 持ち主 *mochinushi*

## P

pagoda 塔 *toh*

painful 痛い *itai*

painkiller 鎮痛剤 *chintsuuzai*

painter 画家 *gaka*

painting 絵/絵画 *e/kai ga*

pair 一組 *hitokumi*

paper 紙 *kami*

paralysed 麻痺した *mahishita*

parcel 小包 *kozutsumi*

parent 親 *oya*

» *(mother)* 母親 *haha oya*

» *(father)* 父親 *chichi oya*

parents 両親 *ryohshin*

park 公園 *kohen*

» national park 国立公園 *kokuritsu kohen*

partner 伴侶/パートナー *hanryo/pahtonah*

party パーティー *pahtii*

» *(political)* 政党 *seitoh*

to pass *(on road)* 通り過ぎます *tohrisugimas*

» *(salt etc.)* 渡します *watashimas*

» *(exam, test)* 合格します *gohkaku shimas*

passenger 乗客 *johkyaku*

past 過去 *kako*

» in the past 昔は *mukashi wa*

path 道/通り道 *michi/tohri michi*

patient 我慢強い *gaman zuyoi*

» *(at hospital)* 患者 *kanja*

pattern 傾向/パターン *keikoh/patahn*

» *(decorative)* 模様 *mo yoh*

**pavement** 歩道 hodoh
**to pay** 支払います shiharaimas
**peak** 山頂 sanchoh
**pen** ペン pen
» **fountain pen** 万年筆 mannenshitsu
**pencil** 鉛筆 enpitsu
**peninsula** 半島 hantoh
**pension** 年金 nenkin
**pensioner** 年金生活者 nenkin
　seikatsusha
**people** 人々 hitobito
**pepper** こしょう koshoh
**perfume** 香水 kohsui
**period** (menstrual) 生理 seiri
» **period pains** 生理痛 seiritsuu
**permit** 許可 kyoka
**to permit** 許可します kyoka shimas
**person** 人 hito
**personal** 個人の kojin no
**petrol** ガソリン gasorin
**photocopy** コピー kopii
**photo** 写真 shashin
**photographer** 写真家/カメラマン
　shashinka/kameraman
**phrase book** 慣用表現集/会話表
　現集 kanyoh hyogen shuu/kaiwa
　hyogen shuu
**pickles** 漬物 tsukemono
**pillow** 枕 makura
**place** 場所 basho
**plan** 計画 keikaku
**plane** 飛行機 hikohki
**plastic bag** ビニール袋 biniiru bukuro
**plate** お皿 osara
**play** 遊び asobi
» (theatre) 芝居 shibai
**to play** (have fun) 遊びます asobimas
» (sport) 競技をします kyogi o shimas
» (musical instruments) 演奏をします
　ensoh o shimas
**pleased** 嬉しい ureshii
» **pleased to meet you** お会いできて
　嬉しいです oai dekite ureshii des
**plenty (of)** たくさんの takusan no

**plug** (bath) 栓 sen
» (electrical) 差込み sashikomi
**poisonous** 有毒な yuudoku na
**police** 警察 keisatsu
» **police station** 警察署 keisatsu sho
**polite** 丁寧な teinei na
**politician** 政治家 seijika
**political** 政治の seijino
**politics** 政治 seiji
**polluted** 汚染された osen sareta
**pollution** 汚染 osen
**poor** 貧しい mazushii
**popular** 人気のある ninki no aru
**portable** 携帯用の keitaiyoh no
**portion** 取り分/量 toribun/ryoh
**portrait** 肖像画 shohzohga
**possible** 可能な kanoh na
**to post** 郵便で送ります yuubin de
　okurimas
**postbox** 郵便受け yuubin uke
**postcard** はがき hagaki
**pound** (sterling) ポンド pondo
**to pour** つぎます tsugimas
**powder** 粉 kona
**power** (electricity) 電源 dengen
» (strength) 力 chikara
**power cut** 停電 teiden
**powerful** 強い tsuyoi
**prefecture** 県 ken
**pregnant** 妊娠している ninshin
　shiteiru
**to prepare** 準備します junbi shimas
**to present** 贈ります okurimas
**pretty** (cute) かわいい kawaii
**price** 値段 nedan
**priest** 僧侶 sohryo
» (in Shinto) 神主 kannushi
**prime minister** 内閣総理大臣/首相
　naikaku sohri daijin/shushoh
**to print** 印刷します insatsu shimas
**prison** 刑務所 keimusho
**private** 個人的な kojinteki na
**prize** 賞 shoh

probably おそらく/たぶん *osoraku/ tabun*

problem 問題 *mondai*

product 製品 *seihin*

profession 職業 *shokugyoh*

professional 専門家/プロ *senmonka/ puro*

professor (大学) 教授 *(dai gaku) kyohju*

profit 利益 *rieki*

programme プログラム *puroguramu*

» (TV, radio) 番組 *bangumi*

to promise 約束します *yakusoku shimas*

to pronounce 発音します *hatsuon shimas*

properly きちんと *kichinto*

property 不動産/財産 *fudohsan/ zaisan*

proud 誇りに思う *hokori ni omou*

public 公共の *kohkyoh no*

to pull 引きます *hikimas*

puppetry 人形芝居 *ningyoh shibai*

pure 純粋な *junsui na*

purple 紫の *murasaki no*

purse 財布 *saifu*

to push 押します *oshimas*

» push-chair ベビーカー *bebii kah*

to put 置きます *okimas*

» to put on 身に着けます *mi ni tsuke mas*

pyjamas パジャマ *pajama*

» (Japanese) 寝巻き *nemaki*

## Q

quality 品質 *hinshitsu*

quantity 量 *ryoh*

quarter 四分の一 *yon bun no ichi*

queen 女王 *johoh*

question 質問 *shitsumon*

queue 列 *retsu*

quickly 急いで *isoide*

quiet 静かな *shizukana*

quite けっこう *kekkoh*

## R

rabbit うさぎ *usagi*

radio ラジオ *rajio*

radioactivity 放射能 *hohshanoh*

radio station ラジオ放送局 *rajio hohsoh kyoku*

railway station 駅 *eki*

rain 雨 *ame*

» it's raining 雨が降っています *ame ga futte imas*

rare 珍しい *mezurashii*

» (steak) レア *rea*

rash 軽率な *keisotsu na*

raw 生の *nama no*

razor かみそり *kamisori*

to read 読みます *yomimas*

reading 読書 *dokusho*

ready (authentic) 準備が出来た *junbi ga dekita*

real (authentic) 本当の *hontoh no*

really 本当に *hontoh ni*

» is it really? 本当ですか? *hontoh des ka*

rear 後ろ *ushiro*

reason 理由 *riyuu*

receipt 領収書 *ryohshuusho*

to receive 受け取ります *uketorimas*

reception 受付 *uketsuke*

to recognise わかります/認めます *wakarimas/mitomemas*

to recommend 勧めます *susume mas*

to record 記録します *kiroku shimas*

to recover 回復します *kaifuku shimas*

red 赤/赤い *aka/akai*

to reduce 減らします *herashi mas*

refund 払い戻し *harai modoshi*

region 地域 *chiiki*

regional 地方の *chihoh no*

to register 登録します *tohroku shimas*

registered post 書留郵便 *kakitome yuubin*

regular いつもの *itsumono*

relationship 関係 *kankei*

religion 宗教 *shuukyoo*

to remain 残ります *nokorimas*

to remember 覚えています oboete imas
to remove 取り除きます torinozoki mas
to rent 借ります karimas
to repair 修理します shuuri shimas
to repeat 繰り返します kurikaeshi mas
to reply 返事をします/答えます henji o shimas/kotaemas
to request 頼みます tanomimas
to rescue 救助します kyuujo shimas
reserved 予約済みの yoyakuzumi no
to rest 休みます yasumimas
result 結果 kekka
retired 退職した taishoku shita
to return (person) 帰ります kaerimas
» (something) 返します kaeshimas
reverse-charge call コレクトコール korekuto kohru
rice (uncooked) 米 kome
» (cooked) ご飯 gohan
» to boil/steam rice ご飯を炊きます gohan o takimas
rice bowl 茶碗 chawan
rice cake 餅 mochi
rice cracker 煎餅 senbei
rich 金持ちの kanemochi no
to ride (bike, horse) 乗ります norimas
right 右 migi
» (correct) 正しい tadashii
ring (jewellery) 指輪 yubiwa
ring (in sumo) 土俵 dohyoh
ripe 熟した jukushita
risk 危険 kiken
river 川 kawa
road 道路 dohro
roadworks 道路工事 dohro kohji
robbery 強盗 gohtoh
rock (music) ロック rokku
roof 屋根 yane
room 部屋 heya
rotten 腐った kusatta
rough (sea) 荒れた areta
» (surface) ざらざらした zara zara shita
round 丸い marui

royal 王室の/王立の ohshitsu no/ ohritsu no
rubbish ごみ gomi
rucksack リュックサック ryukku sakku
rude 失礼な shitsurei na
to run 走ります hashiri mas
rush hour ラッシュアワー rasshu awah
rusty さびた sabita

## S

sad 悲しい kanashii
safe 安全な anzen na
» (strongbox) 金庫 kinko
sake cup 杯 sakazuki
sake pourer とっくり tokkuri
salt 塩 shio
salty 塩辛い shio karai
same 同じ onaji
sample 見本 mihon
sand 砂 suna
sandals サンダル sandaru
» (Japanese) 下駄 geta 草履 zohri
sanitary towel 生理用ナプキン seiri yoh napukin
sash (for kimono) 帯 obi
saucer 受け皿 uke zara
to say 言います ii mas
to scald やけどをします yakedo o shimas
scales はかり hakari
scarf (long) マフラー mafurah
» (square) スカーフ sukahfu
» (Japanese) 風呂敷き furoshiki
scenery 景色 keshiki
school 学校 gakkoh
» crammer 塾 juku
science 科学 kagaku
scissors はさみ hasami
score 得点 tokuten
» what's the score? 得点は何点ですか? tokuten wa nanten des ka

Scotland スコットランド sukotto
rando

Scottish スコットランドの sukotto
rando no

» (person) スコットランド人 sukotto
rando jin

sculpture 彫刻 chohkoku

sea 海 umi

seal (Japanese) 印鑑/判 inkan/han

seasickness 船酔い funa yoi

season 季節 kisetsu

seat 席 seki

secretary 秘書 hisho

» Secretary 大臣 daijin

to see 見ます mimas

to sell 売ります urimas

to send 送ります okurimas

senior 先輩/上級の senpai/johkyuno

senior citizen 高齢者 kohreisha

senior high school 高等学校/高校
kohtoh gakkoh/kohkoh

» student/s 高校生 kohkohsei

sensible 良識のある ryoshiki no aru

sentence 文 bun

separately 別々に betsu betsu ni

serious 本気の honki no

» are you serious? 本気ですか?
honki des ka

sewing 裁い物 nuimono

sex (gender) 性別 seibetsu

» (intercourse) セックス sekkusu

shade かげ kage

shampoo シャンプー shanpuu

sharp (edge) 鋭い surudoi

» (pain) 激しい hageshii

to shave そります sorimas

shaving cream/foam シェービング
クリーム sheibingu kuriimu

she 彼女は/が kanojo wa/ga

sheet (for bed) シーツ shiitsu

» (paper) 用紙 yohshi

shellfish 貝 kai

shirt ワイシャツ waishatsu

shock (electrical) 感電 kanden

» (emotional) ショック shokku

shoe(s) 靴 kutsu

» shoe size 靴のサイズ kutsu no
saizu

shoe repairer 靴修理 kutsu shuuri

shop assistant 店員 tenin

short 短い mijikai

» (person) 背が低い se ga hikui

to shout 大声を出します ohgoe o
dashimas

to show 見せます misemas

shrine 神社 jinja

to shut しめます shimemas

» shut up! 黙れ damare!

shy 内気な/恥ずかしがりの
uchikina/hazukashi garino

sick 病気の byohki no

side 側面 sokumen

sightseeing 観光 kankoh

sign 表示/サイン hyohji/sain

to sign 署名します/サインをします
shomei shimas/sain o shimas

signal 信号 shingoh

signature 署名/サイン shomei/sain

silence 静けさ shizukesa

silk 絹/シルク kinu/shiruku

silver 銀/シルバー gin/shirubah

similar 似ている niteiru

simple 簡単な kantan na

since 一以来/-から -irai/-kara

to sing 歌います utaimas

single (unmarried) 独身の dokushin no

to sit (down) 座ります suwari mas

» to sit down cross-legged あぐらを
かきます agura o kakimas

site 場所/現場 basho/genba

» historic site 史跡 shiseki

size (clothes, shoes) 大きさ/サイズ
ohkisa/saizu

skates (ice) アイススケート aisu
sukeito

» (roller) ローラースケート rohrah
sukeito

**ski boots** スキー靴 *sukii gutsu*

**skiing** スキー *sukii*

**ski-lift** (スキー)リフト *(sukii) rifuto*

**skin** 皮膚 *hifu*

**skirt** スカート *sukahto*

**sky** 空 *sora*

**to sleep** 寝ます/眠ります *nemas/nemu rimas*

**sleeping bag** 寝袋 *nebukuro*

**sleeve** そで *sode*

**slice** 一切れ/一枚 *hitokire/ichimai*

**sliding door** 引き戸 *hikido*

» **sliding screen door** ふすま *fusuma*

**slim** 細い/スマートな *hosoi/sumahto na*

**slipper** (indoor) スリッパ/上履き *surippa/uwabaki*

» (outdoor) 下履き *shitabaki*

**slow** 遅い *osoi*

**to slow down** スピードを落とします *supii do o otoshimas*

**small** 小さい *chiisai*

**smell** におい *nioi*

**smile** 笑顔 *egao*

**smoke** 煙 *kemuri*

**to smoke** たばこを吸います *tabako o suimas*

**smooth** 滑らかな *nameraka na*

**to sneeze** くしゃみをします *kushami o shimas*

**snow** 雪 *yuki*

**to snow** 雪が降ります *yuki ga furimas*

» **it's snowing** 雪が降っています *yuki ga futte imas*

**soap** 石けん *sekken*

» **soap opera** ホームドラマ *hohmu dorama*

**society** 社会 *shakai*

**socks** 靴下 *kutsushita*

**soft** 柔らかい *yawarakai*

**software** ソフトウェア *sofuto uea*

**soldier** 兵士 *heishi*

**sold out** 売り切れ *urikire*

**solid** 固体の *kotaino*

**to solve** 解決します *kaiketsu shimas*

**some** いくらかの *ikuraka no*

**somehow** なんとかして *nantoka shite*

**someone** 誰か *dareka*

**something** 何か *nanika*

**sometimes** 時々 *tokidoki*

**somewhere** どこかで *dokoka de*

**son** 息子 *musuko*

**song** 歌 *uta*

**soon** まもなく *mamonaku*

» **as soon as possible** 出来るだけ早く *dekirudake hayaku*

**sore** (painful) 痛い *itai*

**sorry** (regret) 残念な *zannen na*

**sound** 音 *oto*

**sour** 酸っぱい *suppai*

**south** 南 *minami*

**souvenir** おみやげ *omiyage*

**space** 空間 *kuukan*

**spare time** 余暇 *yoka*

**to speak** 話します *hanashimas*

**special** 特別な *tokubetsu na*

**specialist** 専門家 *senmonka*

**speed** 速度/スピード *sokudo/supiido*

**to spend** (money) 使います *tsukaimas*

» (time) 過ごします *sugoshimass*

**spice** 薬味/スパイス *yakumi/supaisu*

**spider** くも *kumo*

**spoon** スプーン *supuun*

**sport** スポーツ *supohtsu*

**to sprain** 捻挫します *nenza shimas*

**spring** 春 *haru*

**square** (shape) 四角 *shikaku*

**stairs** 階段 *kaidan*

**to stand** 立ちます *tachimas*

**star** 星 *hoshi*

**to stare** じろじろ見ます *jiro jiro mimas*

**start** 始まり *hajimari*

**statue** 像 *zoh*

**to stay** (remain) -のままでいます *- no mama de imas*

**to steal** 盗みます *nusumimas*

**steep** 急な *kyuu na*

step (stairs) 階段 *kaidan*
sticky ねばねばした *neba neba shita*
stiff 堅い *katai*
still (yet) まだ *mada*
to sting 刺します *sashimas*
stock exchange 株式取引 *kabu shiki torihiki*
stolen 盗まれた *nusumareta*
stomach 胃／おなか *i/onaka*
stone 石 *ishi*
to stop (moving) 止まります *tomarimas*
stop! 止まれ *tomare!*
storey 階 *kai*
story 話／物語 *hanashi/mono gatari*
straight まっすぐな *massugu na*
 » straight on まっすぐ *massugu*
strange 変な *henna*
straw わら *wara*
 » (drinking) ストロー *sutoroh*
strike (at) 攻撃／ストライキ *kohgeki/sutoraiki*
 » to go on strike ストライキをします *sutoraiki o shimas*
string ひも *himo*
strong 強い *tsuyoi*
student 学生 *gakusei*
to study 勉強します *benkyoh shimas*
stupid ばかな *baka na*
style (type) スタイル／型 *sutairu/kata*
subtitle 字幕 *jimaku*
suburb 郊外 *kohgai*
to succeed 成功します *seikoh shimas*
success 成功 *seikoh*
suddenly 突然 *totsuzen*
summer 夏 *natsu*
sumo grand champion 横綱 *yokozuna*
sun 太陽 *taiyoh*
to sunbathe 日光浴をします *nikkohyoku o shimas*
sunglasses サングラス *sangurasu*
sunstroke 日射病 *nisshabyoh*
surprised 驚いた *odoroita*
to swallow 飲み込みます *nomikomimas*

to sweat 汗さかきます *ase o kakimas*
sweet 甘い *amai*
sweets (Japanese) 和菓子 *wagashi*
to swell はれます *haremas*
to swim 泳ぎます *oyogimas*
swimming trunks 海水パンツ *kaisui pantsu*
swimsuit 水着 *mizugi*
switch スイッチ *suicchi*
to switch off 消します *keshimas*
to switch on つけます *tsukemas*
sword 刀 *katana*
symptom 症状 *shohjoh*

T
table テーブル *teiburu*
to take 持って行きます *motteikimas*
 » (exam) 試験を受けます *shiken o ukemas*
 » (photo) 写真を撮ります *shashin o torimas*
 » (time) 時間がかかります *jikan ga kakarimas*
to take off (clothes) 脱ぎます *nugimas*
 » (plane) 離陸します *ririku shimas*
to talk 話します *hanashimas*
tall 背が高い *se ga takai*
tap 蛇口 *jaguchi*
tap water 水道水 *suidohsui*
taste 味 *aji*
tattoo 入れ墨 *irezumi*
tax 税金 *zeikin*
taxi タクシー *takushii*
 » taxi rank タクシー乗り場 *takushii noriba*
tea 紅茶 *kohcha*
 » barley tea 麦茶 *mugicha*
 » green tea お茶／緑茶 *ocha/ryokucha*
 » powdered green tea 抹茶 *maccha*
tea cup (Japanese) 湯呑み *yunoni*
to teach 教えます *oshiemas*
teacher 教師 *kyohshi*
 » (form of address) 先生 *sensei*

teapot *(for Japanese tea)* きゅうす *kyuusu*

» *(for English tea)* ティーポット *tii potto*

**technical** 技術的な *gijyutsuteki na*

**technology** 科学技術 *kagaku gijyutsu*

**telephone** 電話 *denwa*

**to telephone** 電話をかけます *denwa o kakemas*

**television** テレビ *terebi*

**to tell** 伝えます *tsuta e mas*

**temperature** 温度 *ondo*

**to have a temperature** 熱があります *netsu ga arimas*

**temple** 寺/寺院 *tera/jiin*

**terrible** ひどい *hidoi*

**textbook** テキスト *tekisuto*

**text message** メール *meiru*

**thank you very much** どうもありがとうございます *dohmo arigatoh gozaimas*

**that (one)** それ *sore*

» **that one over there** あれ *are*

**theft** 窃盗 *settoh*

**their** 彼/彼女らの *kare/kanojo rano*

**theirs** 彼/彼女らのもの *kare/kanojo rano mono*

**then** その時 *sonotoki*

**there** そこに/で/へ *soko ni/de/e*

**these** この/これらの *kono/korerano*

**they** 彼ら/彼女ら/それら *karera/kanojora/sorera*

**thick** 厚い *atsui*

**thief** 泥棒 *doroboh*

**thin** 薄い *usui*

**thing** 物 *mono*

**to think** 考えます *kangae mas*

» **I (don't) think so** そう思います（思いません） *soh omoi mas (omoi ma sen)*

**thirsty** のどが渇いた *nodo ga kawaita*

**this (one)** これ *kore*

**those (ones)** それ/それら *sore/sorera*

» **those ones over there** あれ/あれら *are/arera*

**thread** 糸 *ito*

**to throw** 投げます *nagemas*

» **to throw away** 捨てます *sutemas*

**thunder** 雷 *kaminari*

**tidy** きちんとした *kichintoshita*

**tie** ネクタイ *nekutai*

**tight** きつい *kitsui*

**till** *(until)* 〜まで *-made*

**time** 時間 *jikan*

» *(frequency)* 度/回 *do/kai*

**timetable** 時刻表 *jikokuhyoh*

**tinned** 缶詰の *kan zume no*

» **tinned tuna** ツナ缶 *tsunakan*

**tin opener** 缶切り *kankiri*

**tired** 疲れた *tsukareta*

**tissues** ティッシュ *tisshu*

**to** 〜へ *e*

**toast** トースト *tohsuto*

» **drink a toast to ...** …に乾杯します *…ni kanpai shimas*

**today** 今日 *kyoh*

**toilet paper** トイレットペーパー *toiretto peipah*

**tonight** 今晩 *konban*

**toothpaste** 歯磨き粉 *hamigakiko*

**toothpick** つまようじ *tsuma yohji*

**top** *(mountain)* 頂上 *chohjoh*

» **on top of** 〜の上に *- no ue ni*

**to touch** 触ります *sawarimas*

**tourist** 観光客 *kankohkyaku*

**tournament** トーナメント *tohnamento*

**town** 町/市 *machi/shi*

» **town hall** 市役所 *shiyakusho*

**toy** おもちゃ *omocha*

**traditional** 伝統的な *dentohteki na*

**traffic lights** 信号 *shingoh*

**to translate** 翻訳します *honyaku shimas*

**translation** 翻訳 *honyaku*

**to travel** 旅行します *ryokoh shimas*

**travel agency** 旅行代理店 *ryokoh dairiten*

**travel sickness** 乗り物酔い *norimono yoi*

**traveller** 旅行者 *ryokohsha*

tree 木 *ki*

triangle 三角 *sankaku*

trouble 困難 *konnan*

trousers ズボン *zubon*

true 本当の *hontoh no*

» **that's true** それは本当です *sore wa hontoh des*

to try やってみます *yatte mimas*

to try on 試着します *shichaku shimas*

tunnel トンネル *tonneru*

turn 順番 *junban*

» **it's my turn** 私の番です *watashi no ban des*

to turn off 消します *keshi mas*

» **to turn on** つけます *tsuke mas*

twice 二度/二回 *nido/nikai*

twins 双子 *futago*

type *(sort)* 種類 *shurui*

to type タイプします *taipu shimas*

typical 典型的な *tenkeiteki na*

## U

ugly 醜い *minikui*

ulcer 潰瘍 *kaiyoh*

umbrella 傘 *kasa*

uncle おじ *oji*

uncomfortable 心地よくない *kokochi yokunai*

under −の下に *-no shita ni*

underground *(subway)* 地下鉄 *chikatetsu*

underground shopping street 地下街 *chikagai*

to understand わかります *wakarimas*

underwater 水中の *suichuu no*

underwear 下着 *shitagi*

to undress 脱ぎます *nugimas*

unemployment 失業 *shitsugyoh*

unfortunately 残念ながら *zannen nagara*

unhappy 不幸な/うれしくない *fukohna/ureshikunai*

uniform 制服 *seifuku*

universe 宇宙 *uchuu*

university 大学 *daigaku*

» **university student** 大学生 *daigakusei*

unlimited 無制限の *museigen no*

unpleasant 不愉快な *fuyukai na*

unreserved seat 自由席 *jiyuu seki*

until −まで *-made*

unusual 珍しい *mezurashii*

unwell 具合が悪い *guai ga warui*

up 上に *ue ni*

urgent 緊急の *kinkyuu no*

urine 尿 *nyoh*

us 私たちを/に *watashi tachi o/ni*

USA アメリカ合衆国/米国 *amerika gasshuu koku/beikoku*

to use 使います *tsukaimas*

useful 役に立つ *yaku ni tatsu*

useless 役に立たない *yaku ni tatanai*

usually たいてい *taitei*

## V

vacant 空いている *aiteiru*

valid 有効な *yuukoh na*

valuable 貴重な *kichoh na*

valuables 貴重品 *kichoh hin*

vase 花瓶 *kabin*

vegetarian 菜食主義の *saishoku shugi no*

» **(person)** ベジタリアン *bejitarian*

very とても *totemo*

to view 眺めます *nagamemas*

» **cherry blossom viewing** 花見 *hana mi*

village 村 *mura*

visa ビザ/査証 *biza/sashoh*

to visit 訪問します/訪ねます *hohmon shimas/tazune mas*

visitor 訪問者 *hohmon sha*

vitamin ビタミン *bitamin*

voice 声 *koe*

voltage 電圧 *denatsu*

to vomit 吐きます *hakimas*

to vote 投票します *tohhyoh shimas*

**wage** 賃金 *chingin*

**to wait (for)** 待ちます *machimas*

**waiting room** 待合室 *machiai shitsu*

**Wales** ウェールズ *ueiruzu*

**to walk** 歩きます *arukimas*
» **go for a walk** 散歩します *sanpo shimas*

**wallet** 財布 *saifu*

**to want** ほしいです *hoshii des*
» **(to do something)** −したいです *-shitai des*

**war** 戦争 *sensoh*

**ward** 区 *ku*

**warm** 暖かい *atatakai*

**to wash** 洗います *araimas*

**washing** 洗濯 *sentaku*

**to watch** 見ます *mimas*

**watch out!** 気をつけて *ki o tsukete!*

**water** 水 *mizu*
» **hot water** お湯 *oyu*
» **boiling water** 熱湯 *nettoh*

**waterfall** 滝 *taki*

**waterproof** 防水の *bohsui no*

**wave** 波 *nami*

**way (method)** 方法 *hohhoh*
» **(path)** 道 *michi*
» **that way** そちらへ *sochira e*
» **that way over there** あちらへ *achira e*
» **this way** こちらへ *kochira e*

**we** 私たちは/が *watashi tachi wa/ga*

**weak (drink)** 薄い *usui*

**weather** 天気 *tenki*

**weather forecast** 天気予報 *tenki yohoh*

**wedding** 結婚式 *kekkon shiki*

**week** 週 *shuu*

**weekday** 平日 *heijitsu*

**weekend** 週末 *shuu matsu*

**weekly** 毎週 *maishuu*

**to weigh** 重さを量ります *omo sa o hakarimas*

**weight** 重さ *omosa*

» **(body)** 体重 *taijuu*

**to welcome** 歓迎します *kangei shimas*

**well** 良く *yoku*

**Welsh** ウェールズの *ueiruzu no*
» **(the Welsh)** ウェールズ人 *ueiruzu jin*

**west** 西 *nishi*
» **the West** 西洋 *seiyoh*

**western** 西の *nishi no*
» **(film)** 西部劇 *seibugeki*

**wet** ぬれた *nureta*

**what?** 何? *nani*

**wheat** 小麦 *komugi*

**when?** いつ? *itsu*

**where?** どこ? *doko*

**which?** どの? *dono*

**which one?** どれ? *dore*

**white** 白/白い *shiro/shiroi*

**who?** 誰/どなた *dare/donata*

**whole** 全部の *zenbu no*

**whose?** 誰の? *dare no*

**why?** どうして *dohshite*

**wide** 広い *hiroi*

**wild** 野生の *yasei no*

**to win** 勝ちます *kachimas*
» **who won?** 誰が勝ちましたか? *dare ga kachimashita ka*

**wind** 風 *kaze*

**window** 窓 *mado*

**windy** 風の強い *kaze no tsuyo i*

**wing** 翼/羽 *tsubasa/hane*

**winter** 冬 *fuyu*

**with** −と一緒に *-to issho ni*

**without** −なしで *-nashi de*

**woman** 女の人/婦人 *onna no hito/fujin*

**wonderful** 素敵な *suteki na*

**woods** 森 *mori*

**wool** ウール *uuru*

**word** 言葉/単語 *kotoba/tango*

**work** 仕事 *shigoto*

**to work (function)** 作動します *sadoh shimas*
» **(job)** 働きます *hatarakimas*

world 世界 *sekai*

to worry 心配します *shinpai shimas*

worse もっと悪い *motto warui*

worth 価値 *kachi*
>> it's not worth it その価値はありません *sono kachi wa arimasen*

to wrap 包みます *tsutsu mimas*

to write 書きます *kakimas*

wrong 間違った *machigatta*

# X

x-ray レントゲン写真 *rentogen shashin*

# Y

to yawn あくびをします *akubi o shimas*

year 年 *toshi/nen*

yellow 黄色 *kiiro*

yen 円 *en*

yes はい *hai*

yesterday きのう *kinoh*

yet まだ *mada*

you (sing.) あなた *anata*
>> (pl.) あなたたち *anata tachi*

young 若い *wakai*

your あなたの/あなたたちの *anata no/anata tachino*

yours あなたの *anata no*

yourself あなた自身 *anata jishin*

youth 若者 *wakamono*

# Z

zen (Buddhism) 禅宗 *zenshuu*

zone 地帯/ゾーン *chitai/zohn*

zoo 動物園 *dohbutsuen*